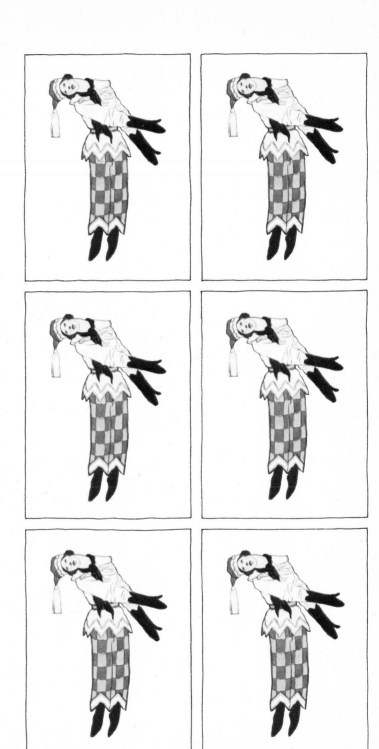

The performing world of the dancer

The performing world of the dancer

Craig Dodd

with a profile of
Anthony Dowell

Silver Burdett Company

Designed and produced by Breslich & Foss, London

Design: Leslie & Lorraine Gerry
Picture Research: Mary Corcoran
House Editor: Nicholas Robinson
Interviews with Anthony Dowell, Patrick Hinson and Pattie Hammond:
Craig Dodd
Interview with Ken Rinker: Deborah Waroff

© Breslich & Foss

Published in the United States
by Silver Burdett Company, © 1981

Library of Congress Catalog Card Number: 8150298
ISBN 0-382-06590-5

Filmset and printed in Great Britain by
BAS Printers Limited

Contents

A World of Dance

1

Early Dancers

Dancers have existed since the earliest times. There are paintings, scrolls, carvings and other records dating back to the beginning of written history and even further which depict dancers. How or why dancing began is unknown, but it is one of the most ancient of the performing arts and has evolved over the years into a sophisticated and exciting form of expression.

Even the ancient Egyptians had dancers and some of the earliest records of dance and music are in the wall-paintings they left in their tombs. There are paintings of harpists and other musicians, as well as of troupes of dancing girls, in the tomb of Tutankhamun. They are, however, in the flat, two-style typical of Egyptian art, so we do not know how the dancers really performed. (The great Russian dancer, Nijinsky, was inspired by Egyptian paintings to create his ballet *Afternoon of a Faun* in that 'flat'

A scene from Nijinsky's ballet *Afternoon of a Faun* showing clearly the two-dimensional poses he used

style: the dancers moving with 'turned-in' feet, sideways to the audience although the Egyptians themselves almost certainly did not dance in that way.)

In ancient Greece, the philosopher Socrates taught that an ability to dance was necessary to acquire grace and elegance. Nevertheless his dance teacher would have been no more than a glorified servant, for though dance was an attractive and desirable skill, it was not considered a respectable profession. Likewise in the Middle Ages, indeed up to the present century, ballet would have been thought of as no more respectable a career than acting. Despite this general attitude, almost every country in the world has a long tradition of dance.

There is strong evidence of how people danced in many fine statues and carvings found in India and Sri Lanka, which show poses used for over two thousand years. Although these dances are not common in the world of the dancer today they are occasionally performed in theatres without a great many changes.

Dancing in the East
Much oriental dancing has a great importance in everyday life. If you see, for example, a Kathakali troupe from South India on stage you will not see the whole performance. If you go into the theatre long before it is time to start, you will see the dancers doing a very complicated ritual of make-up and exercises, and such ritual even extends to the preparation of a meal. The dance company is a whole way of life and is looked after by a guru, a teacher who takes the part of choreographer and recruits and trains young dancers. These dancers must learn a vast range of facial gestures, mime and drama as well as music. They are always men and boys as it is forbidden for women to take part in the Kathakali dance-dramas. The exciting stories of gods and demons were once a way of passing on religious knowledge to a simple population, in much the same way as Italian painters told religious stories in their pictures.

In China and Japan there has always been a highly theatrical element in dance. In China, the famous Opera is highly stylized and its stars have to be

A scene from the popular Kabuki play *The Forty-Seven Ronin*. First staged in 1748 as a puppet play, this story of men's loyalty to their Lord and the ritual of an honourable death was adapted for the Kabuki stage and continues to be performed today

equally adept at dance, mime, singing and acting. Western-style classical ballet has become popular over the last twenty years and the Peking Ballet presents a repertoire including the classics. There were difficult days for the troupe's dancers during the Cultural Revolution of the 1960s when they were sent to work in fields and factories, but the company is now together again under its strong director, Dai Ai-Lan. She is planning to introduce more western ballets as well as choreographers and teachers, though they will continue to dance their own revolutionary ballets such as *The Red Detachment of Women*, which, in the Chinese tradition is extremely long. The dancers have strong techniques and catch the classical style exactly. In fact, one of the most interesting aspects of watching them rehearse is seeing how similar they are to other ballet companies.

In Japan, professional companies have performed Noh plays and Kabuki for several centuries. The earliest dance form was Bugaku but it was performed only for very restricted audiences in the court or shrine. The twentieth-century choreographer George Balanchine was inspired by it to create his own ballet *Bugaku* for his New York City Ballet, but of course this was not an exact recreation of the ancient style.

From Bugaku, the Noh play developed. This is not, in fact, a type of dance, but a form of theatre dependent on stylized movements. The plays are usually long traditional stories of samurai and villains and are so serious that during the fifteenth

3

century the performers introduced a shorter comic play in the interval, a sort of commercial break to encourage custom. There is also Kabuki, the most popular Japanese dance form, which is often seen in theatres in the West. It began to take shape at just the same time that ballet was moving from the court to the theatre in the West. Unfortunately, as with many of the Indian temple dancers, the ladies who took part were often more interested in displaying their charms to the audience than expressing the stories. The authorities in Japan banned the performances, therefore, on the grounds that they were indecent, and out of this grew the tradition of boys taking the female roles. Today they are still specially trained to do so.

This is one of the many similarities that recur throughout the history of dance: boys took the female roles, in much the same way that actors did in Shakespeare's plays. There was little communication between nations yet many other coincidences have occurred. Yaqui Indians wore antlers in their dances, just as English Morris dancers did. Kathak dancers stamped their feet in complex rhythms just as the Spanish did and do now in their flamenco dances. English people danced round their maypole, while American Indians, pictured unfairly as savages, danced around their totem pole.

Two Hopi Indians perform their Eagle Dance, one of the many folk dances which use bird or animal movements

Folk Dances

These dances now generally find their way into national folk dance companies which are often a source of patriotic pride. Folk dances are the oldest form of dance and some of the dances mentioned above fall into this class. A few contain traces of dances from thousands of years ago, although many only date back hundreds of years! Some countries as we shall see, have a wealth of national dances, while other have only one or two. Nonetheless they desperately try to make them fill an evening in the theatre, although sometimes it seems the aim is to attract tourists rather than to preserve dances.

While performers who come from the Far East have usually given over their whole lives to their dancing, it is never certain how authentic the dances are of the folk companies from Eastern Europe and Russia. They often provide excellent theatre, however. To be fair, folk dances do need to be adjusted for the theatre and the dancers have to be given some opportunities to try out new steps and characters.

The most famous Russian folk company, and the one which had done most for this type of dance, is the Moiseyev company. Igor Moiseyev was a Russian dancer who was fascinated by folk dancing. He travelled across Russia collecting dances from the many different states which make up the Soviet Union and tried to present original folk dances, but naturally had to make changes for the theatre. A whole evening of one type of dance can be very boring for the audience, as these dances were originally

A performance in a theatre by the young dancers of the Urals Folk Dance Troupe in Perm, Russia

made to be taken part in and not just to be watched. Moiseyev created some dances specially for the company and made them look so authentic that they were taken as real by audiences in Russia. So many dances have been lost that they thought he had somehow rediscovered them instead of inventing them.

The dancers in this company, which is very large and occasionally splits into different units, come from the great ballet schools of Russia. They usually have ballet training, but if they show a particular talent for character dancing they will specialize in this area. The problem for a dancer in a company like this seems to be the repetitiveness of the work. Admittedly dancers in classical companies suffer from a certain amount of boredom as well, but they can look forward to dancing more varied roles or more varied dance styles as they progress. In a folk dance company the dancer will perfect one step or some special trick and do it at every performance. A Georgian dancer, for example, will learn spectacular feats while dancing on point, almost like a classical ballerina, though in fact it is not the tip of the toe which is used. The Georgian ladies glide around in intricate patterns using tiny steps beneath their long full dresses so that they appear to float over the stage. Other men will do typical Cossack tumbling or the dances with very deep knee bends which appear in every Russian dance and in classic ballets like *The Nutcracker* and *The Sleeping Beauty*. The great Russian companies use their national dances in full-length classical ballets such as *Taras Bulba* or *The Stone Flower* and often they are more successful in this setting.

The Birth of Ballet

At some unknown point the steps of European folk dance took two directions. Some dancers took them into popular art and became members of touring troupes dancing and miming to amuse the widest popular audience and may be the forerunners of vaudeville, music-hall or musical. Other steps were taken up by the nobility, who were very conscious of what they looked like and danced with great refinement. Perhaps out of his rivalry, even snobbery, came

Natalia Makarova and
Mikhail Baryshnikov in
the American Ballet
Theater's production of
Giselle, Act I

the artificial, unreal, unscientific and dangerous art of
ballet. By taking dance into the court and performing
it with the necessary manners, airs and graces they
were taking the first steps to creating an organized
dance form, where dancers would be trained under a
carefully codified system which would end up as a
commercial, theatrical art.

The careful teaching of classical ballet, to a system
which has been refined over three centuries, is the
best base for almost every other dance form. If you
want to be a tap-dancer, a modern dancer, or a dancer
in musicals or on television a good basis of classical
ballet is the best you can have. It will increase your
range and teach you how to cope with almost any
dance situation. For this reason this book con-
centrates on this area of dance training. Of course,
you might want to take up Spanish dancing or learn
about various forms of Indian dance in which case
you can get advice from many other sources;
specialist groups who perform or advertisements in
magazines such as *The Dancing Times, Dance
Magazine* or *Dance News*.

Performance for most people means ballet, in an
Opera House or in their local theatre, in a ballet
school or on television. We take it for granted that
dancers mime to each other, that ballerinas stand on
their toes, that handsome princes jump and spin. But
where did it all start? Who took the first steps?

2 The Early World of Ballet

Dancing at Court

What was it like to take part in one of the great court entertainments of the fifteenth and sixteenth centuries? The beautifully illustrated books which record them, probably the most elaborate souvenir programmes ever produced, show scenes of great splendour. Everything looks immaculately organized, the food is sumptuous, the complicated processions perfect. In reality the courtiers, dancers, tumblers and mummers who took part must have had a lot in common with the members of a corps de ballet today: hours of waiting, little reward and the frustration of taking countless, detailed orders.

One of the most famous court entertainments was the *Ballet Comique de la Reine* which Catherine de Medici, Queen of France arranged to celebrate a royal marriage in 1581. An elaborately illustrated book produced a year later gives a very clear idea of the way the occasion was organized, but naturally gives no idea of the way individual dancers saw their work. The occasion is portrayed from the point of view of the dancing master and, more importantly, was intended to impress the monarch to whom Catherine presented it. They would be left in no doubt that she was the supreme impresario of the day! In the same way, other courts would present entertainments to impress ambassadors, visitors and subjects not only to entertain but to instruct. Each scene would have a point to make, sometimes a political one. If a visiting prince watched a scene in which a noble, classical god defeated the force of evil he would have a fair idea of his host's meaning.

During these performances the monarch and his

A famous illustration from the elaborate book produced to commemorate the *Ballet Comique de la Reine*. The monarch and guests in the foreground watch the various scenes taking place around the hall

guest watched from a platform, with the courtiers who were not taking part arranged in tiers around the ballroom or banqueting hall. Hundreds of masked and costumed people would walk in complicated patterns devised by the dancing masters of the age, who travelled from court to court arranging spectacles for courtiers or for equestrian forces. The dancing master would have control of the whole event, refining the everyday dances and manners of the upper classes into a dance form, which was eventually to become ballet, as well as directing the mass movements. These dancing masters wrote down their theories and plans, but they are academic and formal and do not convey the feeling of any of the occasions, probably because the masters were really musicians, in particular violinists. The idea of being a dancer and nothing but a dancer was as yet unknown. They directed rehearsals with their violins, and right up to the beginning of the twentieth century it was the violin, not the piano, that

9

accompanied the ballet class.

As we have no actual record of what it was like to perform, we must use our imagination. The performers normally wore stiff, heavy costumes and towering head-dresses. Light silks and other materials were sometimes used, but only for the grotesque characters or nymphs and water sprites whose parts would be taken by professional entertainers. The heavy brocades and rich decoration of gold thread which encased the dancers allowed only limited leg movements for the ladies, although the men wore tights as part of court dress and so had more freedom of movement. These costumes must have been cumbersome and tiring, particularly since the performers also wore masks for most of the entertainment. These would have been made of wooden frames and leather with towering plumes of ostrich feathers or some other decoration.

If you think that at one of these occasions hundreds of people took part you can also imagine the difficulties of choosing the dancers for each role. A medieval audition must have been extraordinary. The main roles would automatically have been given to the great courtiers in order of precedence, but the lesser courtiers were probably allotted roles just as though they were soldiers being ordered about in the King's army. Possibly news of the planned celebrations would attract travelling troupes of mummers and acrobats who would be given the parts that were not respectable for the courtiers to play; these would include the performers dressed as mermaids who accompanied the fish course or those dressed as wild animals who entered when the meat dish was served.

Apart from coping with his foot soldiers, the dancing master would have to arrange the mounted section. Animals, horses in particular, were a regular feature contributing both interest and excitement. Knights would parade on chargers in their elaborate armour doing complicated routines which have developed into the dressage events of today's horse shows. They have also provided the names of modern ballet steps and manouvres, the best known being the manège. Exotic animals were also used, such as camels and elephants, and they must have presented immense problems, (as someone who has seen Sir

Frederick Ashton's ballet, *La Fille Mal Gardée*, with its little, live horse may know). A wild tiger once escaped during a pageant. There were also other hazards: artificial lakes burst their banks, ships sank and costumes caught fire. Performances would be lit by thousands of candles and flaming torches and all performers were equally open to danger. Charles VI of France had a narrow escape when he and his young friends took part in a masque dressed as apes, for although they took the precaution of banning torches, the King's brother used one to see who the 'apes' were and set fire to them. The King only escaped injury because he was talking to the Duchess of Berry at the time and this thoughtful lady used her vast skirt to put out the flames.

A scene from the entertainment during which King Charles the Sixth of France and his friends were almost killed when their costumes caught fire

When the dancing master had assembled his cast and planned the theme of the various scenes, rehearsals would start. These are as hard to imagine as the audition. It was said that to arrange these works the dancing master had to have as great a knowledge of geometry as of dancing, and he must have had to behave like a General on a battlefield to communicate across vast banqueting halls or court-yards. Nowadays, for similar displays such as the opening of the Olympics or a political rally, a computer is used to work out the complicated patterns. Then, however, there must have been long periods of idle standing around bored, hot and tired under the great costumes.

The actual performances must have been even more exhausting, as they lasted for many hours. The *Ballet Comique de la Reine* started at ten at night and lasted until nearly four o'clock in the morning. There must have been chaos in the kitchens and corridors, the 'backstage' of the performance, and anxious engineers would have been controlling the complicated machinery to lift performers into the air or make dramatic changes of scenery possible. Each course of the banquet would appear from the kitchens, heavily decorated and almost unrecognizable as food, to be borne into the hall with great ceremony. The pictures we have, however, undoubtedly give a glamorous view; the halls must have been smoky and the food more attractive to look at than to eat.

It seems quite natural that the first star performer to appear was a king. In later life he would even be known by the title of one of his greatest roles, the Sun King. Louis XIV of France was a great dancer, if the stories from the time are true and not merely flattery. He was only twelve when he took part in his first ballet and he continued to dance until he grew too stout in early middle age. He regarded dancing as a civilizing influence and expected members of his court to be good at it. Peter the Great of Russia felt the same way and hoped to refine his coarse courtiers by encouraging them to dance. In England, a little later, the much-travelled Lord Chesterfield stressed the importance of dance for good deportment in his celebrated Letters to his son.

The First Academy

When Louis XIV gave up dancing the court also stopped and so became the first audience for paid dancers. Although it still looked like court dance, ballet was on the way to becoming a theatre art. Louis established his Royal Academy to organize the teaching of dance in 1661, for he felt it was important to combine various teachings and to standardize techniques as they developed. (Already small, simple jumps such as the entrechat, cabriole and chassé were being performed by men and women.) The Academy opened its doors as a theatre in 1672 with an opera which contained dances, singing, drama and mime—a type of performance which would last until the end of the following century. The Academy had a variety of homes ranging from a tennis court to a royal palace and developed into the Paris Opéra company which is now housed in a splendid nineteenth-century theatre, also called the Opéra.

Jean-Baptiste Lully, the great composer and arranger of ballets for Louis XIV, gradually introduced court ladies into performances, in parts which had previously been played by boys. Court gentlemen, in turn, were given special permission to partner them without loss of respectability.

A very elaborate scene from a Grand Fête given by Mary, Princess of Orange in the Hague in 1686. Two hundred years after Catherine de Medici's first spectacle the arrangement is still very stiff and formal, though ballet was about to become a theatre art

The first truly professional ballerina to emerge from the Academy was Mlle. de La Fontaine who appeared supported by three other ballerinas. In period illustrations she looks very attractive, but on stage she would have worn or carried a mask. The roles she danced were much the same as those in court entertainments. Her first role in *The Triumph of Love* in 1681 could well have been performed to celebrate a betrothal or marriage at court. She would have worn the stiff bodice and full court skirt which allowed only limited movement. Men also wore a variation of court dress, consisting of a tunic and tights with a stiff short skirt at the waist, curiously like the classical tutu which would appear two centuries later. This costume gave the male dancer more freedom to move and do more exciting steps than his ballerina who could only do small jumps. As turn-out was beginning to be established the male dancer would have the ability to raise his leg slightly to the side which is essential on stage, for without it the performance would have to be done in profile and it would be impossible to turn.

In about 1700 the five positions of the feet were written down by the ballet master Pierre Beauchamps. To achieve more brilliant steps turn-out became essential; so essential that machines were devised to help the dancer. Even as late as the middle of the nineteenth century, when dance training should have made them unnecessary, one dancer wrote of the half hour of daily torture she suffered as she stood in a wooden box forcing her feet into the typical straight line from toe to heel and heel to toe. Even the great ballerina Nathalie FitzJames used to lie on the floor and have her servant stand on her hips. At least she had the right idea; turn-out must come from the hips and not just from the knee down.

The Ballerina

The beginning of the eighteenth century saw the gradual rise of the ballerina to the supreme position she would hold for nearly two hundred years. Françoise Prévost was the greatest ballerina at the turn of the century but she was overshadowed by two of her pupils, Marie-Anne de Cupis de Camargo and

Marie Sallé. Prévost did her best to keep La Camargo in the corps de ballet, but did not succeed, as La Camargo drew attention to herself by jumping on the stage to dance the solo of a male dancer who had failed to appear. The impact was tremendous and her career was launched. Reports say that she was not really pretty, not tall and not shapely for a dancer. Other great dancers appear to have been equally unsuitable at first appearance. The great technician Anna Heinel, who perfected various pirouettes, was described as being a man in woman's guise, and Marie Taglioni was called 'a little hunchback' and it was said she would never learn to dance.

La Camargo's brilliant technique was used to best effect in lively dances to equally lively music. Her fine footwork brought about a most important change as her dress was shortened to show off the steps. This rise of a few inches, for ever immortalised in Nicolas Lancret's painting which is in every ballet book, would lead to the Romantic skirt, the classical tutu, body tights and eventually to nudity, over a period of two hundred and fifty years.

The great lover Casanova, who saw many of the dancers of this period, wrote that La Camargo bounded like a fury, but did not jump high and that, like so many dancers who were vivacious on stage, she was rather sad off-stage.

Prévost's other great pupil, Marie Sallé, had to go to London in order to perform her ballet *Pygmalion* as she wanted to wear light draperies which would have been unthinkable in Paris. Sallé was another vivacious dancer, but she made her impact by her expressive powers and not her technique.

While La Camargo and Sallé were dancing, the first signs of 'balletomania' appeared. Camargo's small feet were universally admired and made a fortune for her shoemaker who sold a 'Camargo Shoe' to ladies who thought they would similarly flatter *their* feet. From these modest beginnings would grow the mania for the Romantic ballerinas which reached levels of complete madness during the early years of the next century. Taglioni's fans did not copy her shoes, but they cooked and ate the last pair she wore in Russia.

The ballerina, however, had not yet outshadowed

Above: Gaetano Vestris the first 'God of the Dance' was also the first dancer to discard the use of a mask

the male dancer and during the next century or so we come across three 'gods of the Dance'. The first was Louis Dupré who had a long dancing career during his seventy-seven years. Casanova saw him late in life, still dancing at the age of sixty, and noted his precision and lightness in spite of the costumes and masks. His mantle was taken over by Gaetano Vestris, equally famous as a dancer and actor, whose life almost spanned the eighteenth century, a century he dominated. When his son, Auguste, succeeded him Gaetano accepted that he was an even greater dancer, but only because he had had *him* as a father.

These dancers usually made their debuts at an early age—Auguste Vestris for instance, was only twelve at his—and had very long careers. But they lived during the age of masks and stylized acting with ballet as only one part of the performance, and although new steps were being developed, dancing was not as physically arduous as it is today. Great leaps or catches, one-handed lifts or multiple fouéttes were far in the future. Even the entrechat would have been performed differently, depending more on the speed of the feet and not on the height of the jump.

The world of ballet would stay much the same until Dauberval put into practice the theories and teachings of his teacher, Jean Georges Noverre, in *La Fille Mal Gardée* in Bordeaux in 1789. This ballet gave the dancer the opportunity to create living characters on the stage, to dance in a natural manner in a performance consisting entirely of dance. Gone were the masks, the spoken drama, the singing and the cumbersome costumes. Ballet was at last born as a theatre art.

The Modern World of Ballet

3

The modern performing world of the ballet dancer really started as long ago as the early years of the nineteenth century and since that time it has changed surprisingly little. Of course there have been dramatic improvements in technique and the range of subject-matter of ballets has widened, but the basics are remarkably similar. The great ballets of that period, *La Sylphide* and *Giselle*, have themselves stood the test of time as well as being the models for many later ballets. Similarly the dancers who created them inspired future generations and formed a style which is still important to all ballet dancers.

The Triumph of the Ballerina

The Romantic Age, which in ballet lasted only about fifteen years from around 1830, marked the rise of the ballerina to a position of supreme importance. The male dancer was in every sense of the word a 'porter', there only to support and carry the ballerina and rarely allowed to display himself in a solo. There were exceptions such as the talented Jules Perrot who started life as a mime at the age of thirteen. As Perrot was so short of stature the great teacher Auguste Vestris, advised him to dance quickly, to dart about so that the audience would not notice his lack of inches or indeed his rather plain features. A master of stagecraft, Vestris also encouraged his ballerinas to be seductive on stage, to be charming and to inspire passion. During the Romantic Age this style of performance would give way to the more austere teaching of Filippo Taglioni who created *La Sylphide* for his daughter, Marie. Taglioni expected

Opposite: Brenda Last and Desmond Kelly of the British Royal Ballet in a scene from Frederick Ashton's *La Fille Mal Gardée*. In 1789 Dauberval produced the original version of this, to different music now lost. It is the first ballet to tell a complete story of everyday people

17

his dancers to be graceful and light and never to use any pose or gesture which lacked modesty. This cool and restrained style is typically Romantic and can be seen to perfection in the second acts of both *Giselle* and *La Sylphide*, the other-worldly 'white' acts.

Marie Taglioni, the greatest ballerina of the age, was the dancer who set the style and the standard; she embodied the ideals of the age. She always gave an impression of such purity and restraint that she was often referred to as a 'Christian' dancer. In contrast the fiery Fanny Elssler was called a 'pagan' dancer. These descriptions, however, were not exactly true as Taglioni often danced colourful and exotic roles, but it suited Dr Veron, the Director of the Paris Opéra, to encourage a little rivalry. He always had an eye for business, as the Opéra was not entirely supported by the state, but his ideas did play a small part in the eventual decline of ballet in Paris. For example he encouraged his pretty young corps de ballet to mix with the rich gentlemen who came to the performances. He even opened up the *foyer de la danse* so that they would have somewhere to meet. As you can guess the gentlemen were not there to see the quality of the ballet! Inevitably while dancers prospered, the dance itself suffered. The social side of the ballet became more important than the dancing and with the exception of one or two great works such as *Coppélia*, ballet in Paris stayed in decline until the beginning of this century. Even in *Coppélia* the part of Franz was played by the most voluptuous ballerina in order to excite the gentlemen in the audience. This soon became a tradition which lasted well into this century.

Another great ballerina of the Romantic Age was Lucile Grahn, the pupil of August Bournonville in Copenhagen. He had his own small world of ballet there, cut off from much else that was happening, and for this we can now be grateful. Alone he encouraged male dancing and created many good roles, often for himself. He also created his *La Sylphide* for Grahn and his is the version you are most likely to see today.

Together with Fanny Cerrito and Carlotta Grisi, Taglioni, Elssler and Grahn were the greatest dancers of the age. They excited public enthusiasm to a pitch that has hardly ever been matched since.

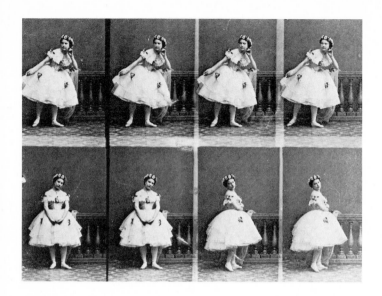

A charming series of photographs of Fanny Cerrito, one of the great Romantic ballerinas, taken when she was almost 40

Elssler had her image engraved on whisky flasks in America. Taglioni had her carriage pulled through the streets by the young noblemen of Vienna. On one occasion she was so thrilled with a new hat that she took it straight from the hat box and wore it immediately. Her hatmaker was horrified when he saw that she had left the brim turned up, which had only been done to protect it from damage in the box. But it was too late. Her public had seen her wearing it and were already having hats with upturned brims made for themselves.

Taglioni's art and style have been captured in many engravings and it is only from these and from written records that we can guess how she performed. She is often shown standing on point, but this could be artistic licence, capturing only the fleeting moment she actually took that position. There were no heavy blocked point shoes in those days and if you look at her shoes in the museum of the Paris Opéra, or those of Lucile Grahn in the Theatre Museum in Copenhagen, you can see that it must have been almost impossible to stay on point for long in them. Although a great dancer Taglioni was not particularly beautiful. When she danced in Russia and attended the Imperial School to do her class the children surrounded her, apparently paying her compliments. In fact they were really saying 'What an ugly mug you've got' and 'How wrinkled you are' while they were smiling at her. Poor Taglioni, not speaking any Russian, was quite overcome and thanked them for their kind words!

These small stories have no real relevance to the art of ballet itself, but they help show what the dancers were like and, even more, the extent to which dance suddenly caught the public's imagination. How popular the ballerinas were is also shown by the fees they were paid. On one occasion in London in 1836, Taglioni demanded, and got, £100, ($240) per performance, as well as extra payments for her father and her brother in various capacities. This was an astronomic sum in those days. When the young Margot Fonteyn started touring almost a hundred years later in 1935 she received £5 a week which she thought was a colossal sum then!

For rewards the size of those offered to Taglioni we

A sketch of Marie Taglioni—less than flattering to her but quite honest

must jump forward a good few years to the height of the Imperial Ballet of the Tsar of Russia. The ballerinas of this company amassed small fortunes in jewels as gifts from various Grand Dukes, suffered the attentions of lovesick poets and played politics influencing government officials. They even tried to browbeat the great Petipa as he worked on his ballets. They demanded bigger solos and threatened to use their influence at court to disgrace him if he did not agree. They forced younger dancers out of roles which might threaten their own position and they wore their real jewels during performances for their admirers to see, not caring if they clashed with the costume design.

Ballet in America

At this time we see the gradual emergence of ballet in America. Fanny Elssler in particular toured America extensively and helped plant the roots of ballet in that country. The tours she undertook must have been hazardous and very hard work. Journeys which now take hours then took days and must have been extraordinarily uncomfortable. The slight inconvenience suffered by today's star dancers flying from continent to continent may amount to no more than the effects of a time-change and swollen feet from the pressurized airplane, bears no comparison to crossing the Atlantic slowly by boat or crossing America by stagecoach or train.

It was at this time that we find what is one of the first ballet companies managed by a ballerina, and it bears a great resemblance to the companies which would later be organized by Anna Pavlova. Augusta Maywood was one of America's earliest ballerinas and was obviously a woman with frontier spirit, for she not only organized her own company, but danced many of the leading roles. Maywood had made her debut in 1837 at the same time as another great American ballerina, Mary Ann Lee. They had both been the pupils of a teacher from the Paris Opéra who was working in Philadelphia. He also taught George Washington Smith who became the partner of Lee and other ballerinas, including the notorious Lola Montez when she appeared in New York in 1851.

Lee made the long journey to Paris to learn *Giselle*

from the choreographer Coralli and returned home to stage the first American performance in 1846. She then formed a touring company with George Washington Smith and presented some ambitious ballets before retiring through ill-health at the early age of twenty-four.

While frontiers were being extended in America and ballet was being taken to a wider audience, the real development of ballet was taking place in Russia.

Petipa and the Rise of Russian Ballet

Russia became the centre of ballet following the decline of dance in Paris immediately after the Romantic Age. The great ballerinas of the time did, of course, continue dancing long after the famous *Pas de Quatre* of 1845, which is often taken as being the end of that era.

Looking for new opportunities, a French dancer called Marius Petipa took the post of principal dancer in St Petersburg in 1847. His career as a dancer before that time had been overshadowed by that of his brother, Lucien, who had partnered the great Romantic ballerinas and also created the role of Albrecht in *Giselle* in 1841. Marius had started as a dancer with his father's company in Brussels, but at an early age had started to create ballets of his own. He continued to dance with various touring groups, and indeed from these tours to places such as Spain, he acquired his knowledge of national dances which he would later use in ballets.

Following the poetry and restraint of the Romantic Age, interest had turned to colourful ballets introducing national dances such as the Czardas and Mazurka or variations on them such as Petipa used in *Don Quixote*.

In 1862 Petipa produced his first ballet in Russia, *The Daughter of the Pharaoh*, and it was such a success that he was offered the post of ballet master, a post he held for forty years. During this time he created over fifty full-length ballets, including the three classics, *The Sleeping Beauty*, *The Nutcracker* and *Swan Lake*. Other famous works include *Raymonda* and *La Bayadère* which are not so often done in full-length versions in the West.

The dancers Petipa worked with were employees of the Tsar's household, part of the civil service like clerks or soldiers. They were there to entertain the court and few outsiders were allowed to see the performances in St Petersburg until near the end of the century. Belonging to the ballet was a sought-after occupation as in a time of great hardship for the mass of the population it provided security and a better standard of living. For the girls it could even provide a rich husband or protector.

Dancers for the company were trained in the well-established Imperial School which had a long and distinguished history dating back to the time of Peter the Great. Over the years it had employed many notable teachers and produced excellent dancers. Interest in ballet increased during the Romantic Era owing to the visits of Marie Taglioni and one of her partners, Christian Johansson, who had worked with Bournonville in Copenhagen. He eventually joined the company and later became a distinguished teacher in the school.

One of Johansson's pupils in later years, in his *Classe de Perfection*, was to be Tamara Karsavina, though by that time he was in his nineties and almost blind. He had taught her father, too. It is from Karsavina's charming biography, *Theatre Street*, that we get a perfect picture of life in the Imperial School, its discipline and its teaching standards. She gives touching descriptions of her entry into the

The second 'white' act of *Swan Lake* as danced by the Bolshoi Ballet of Moscow in 1951. Soviet versions of this ballet often have a 'happy' ending with the Swan Queen being transformed back into a Princess

23

Tamara Karsavina and Vaslav Nijinsky in *Le Spectre de la Rose*, a young girl's dream of her first ball and the perfume of the rose she wore. You can see how Nijinsky's physique is very different from an ideal type today

school, the auditions and tests, as well as the daily life. She also makes interesting comments about the great ballerinas of the day, ballerinas the girls in the school had passions for. She reports first-hand on Pierina Legnani's famous ability to do thirty-two fouettés. She tells us that Legnani was short and not pretty (how often we come across this description of great ballerinas!) and performed the fouettés as though they were a circus trick. She created suspense before performing them. She took time walking very deliberately to the centre of the stage and made a fuss of making her preparation. The conductor would wait, baton at the ready, for her nod before she whirled into the pirouettes.

Karsavina herself was an altogether different dancer, stressing great artistry and poetry in her work. Apart from the quality of her dancing she is important as one of the group of dancers who moved from the last century into this one and from the world of the Imperial Ballet to the exciting world of

Diaghilev and his company in Paris. The other dancers included Pavlova and Vaslav Nijinsky with whom Karsavina would form a great partnership.

Dancers in the Imperial Ballet were very restricted in what they were allowed to do. They had to dance what Petipa gave them and experiment of any kind was discouraged. Of course the ballerinas had wonderful opportunities to create great roles such as Odette/Odile or Aurora, but the soloists and corps de ballet would be allotted a solo or character part strictly in keeping with their position in the company. If you were a soloist you need not expect to be given one step which might outshine the prima ballerina. In the same way young dancers who wanted to create new ballets and experiment with choreography were not encouraged. Petipa had created a formula for his full-length ballets and although this was new and exciting for the first few ballets, he did not really develop it until he retired.

Anna Pavlova in the title role of *Giselle*, the greatest ballet of the Romantic Age

Diaghilev and the Ballets Russes

Mikhail Fokine, a young dancer from the Imperial Ballet was brought into contact with Diaghilev and his friends who wanted to free ballet from Petipa's restrictions. They wanted a new approach: different attitude to decor and much more interesting stories.

The chance came when Diaghilev eventually managed to arrange some performances of ballet during an opera season in Paris in 1909. By this time Fokine had created his first ballets, such as *Les Sylphides*, and his famous solo, *The Dying Swan*, for Anna Pavlova who joined this first tour, but soon left to form her own company with which she would tour the world.

While Diaghilev went on to astound Paris and then the rest of Europe and America, Pavlova toured towns and cities performing ballets created for her and her corps of English girls, who were specially chosen as they were the easiest to control! She would appear almost everywhere, in small towns with awful facilities or places where ballet had never been seen before. She trekked across Australia and New Zealand and even appeared in Japan. She danced in music halls and vaudeville, her ballet items coming in between animal acts and acrobats. This was not so unusual at the time as there just was not the mass audience for ballet necessary to fill the biggest theatres. Even Nijinsky appeared in variety after he left the Diaghilev company.

While Pavlova was creating larger audiences for ballet, Diaghilev was creating artistic opportunities for painters, choreographers, musicians and dancers. He managed to keep his major company in operation, with only minor breaks, for almost twenty years. He begged and charmed money from rich friends, found engagements and bullied managements to keep his artistic group together. He encouraged choreographers to make substantial roles for dancers in place of endless divertissements. What would the world of ballet be like today without the example of *Petrouchka*, *The Firebird*, or the controversial *The Rite of Spring*? In encouraging dancers such as Nijinsky, Massine and others to create ballets he opened up a whole new world. During this period there were, of course, other companies, but the

Serge Diaghilev, founder of the Ballets Russes, who brought together many great dancers, choreographers, composers, painters and designers to create such ballets as *Petrouchka* and *The Firebird*

ballets they were presenting were popular entertainments on the same level as light-hearted operettas, with the exception of the Swedish Ballet of Rolf de Maré, based in Paris.

Ballet Today

With the death of Diaghilev in 1929, when the company was on holiday, we come to the world of ballet as we know it today. With the exception of the Royal Danish Ballet which was quietly going its own way, almost all ballet today can be traced from this point. Even the great Paris Opéra, with its long tradition, took on a new lease of life when Serge Lifar, who had worked with Diaghilev, become director. George Balanchine, also a member of Diaghilev's company, went to America, and other dancers founded schools and small companies in many other places. In the same way many of Pavlova's dancers often stayed behind in places they visited, Australia in particular, to found schools which would eventually become the basis of national companies. Britain had benefited from Diaghilev's example very early on through the work of Marie Rambert and Ninette de Valois, who were later joined by Alicia Markova and Anton Dolin. De Valois formed the Vic-Wells Ballet out of her own school and it was to this school that the young Margot Fonteyn eventually went when she came back to Britain from China.

Ballet, however, was not such a big business as it is today. Fonteyn, for instance, remembers her audition for the Vic-Wells School. She and her mother did not know what was expected of them and did not even bother to take any practise clothes or shoes, so she did some exercises at the barre in her petticoat with bare feet. She was then taken into the school! Compare that with the difficulties of getting into a major school today.

When dancers graduated in the 1930s there were not so many opportunities for them to work full-time in ballet. The great opera house companies offered employment to some, but companies such as the Ballet Rambert or the Vic-Wells in Britain were on a very small scale. Rambert helped her students as best she could, but dancers such as Ashton and Antony

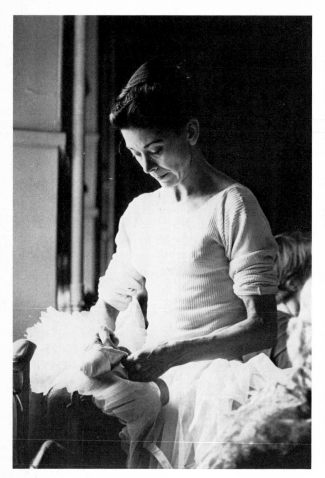

Two great ballerinas, Margot Fonteyn (left) and Maya Plisetskaya (right), doing the regular chore of sewing the toes of their point shoes. This strengthens them and makes them last longer as well as avoiding slipping

Tudor were expected to turn their hand to anything from revue to helping clean the studio. In America, George Balanchine's first company was an extension of the School of American Ballet though they did work with the Metropolitan Opera House and performed ballets, including *Serenade* and *Orpheus and Euridyce.* Apart from small ventures such as Ballet Caravan, for which such basic American works as *Billy the Kid* were produced, there were very few other opportunities for dancers, though these did include small groups formed by some of Pavlova's dancers and partners. Indeed from one of these came one of the earliest American productions of *La Fille Mal Gardée.*

The history of the various Ballet Russes companies

A scene from the Ballet Russes' version of *Petrouchka* with Nijinsky in the title role as the frightened puppet about to be murdered, and Karsavina (standing right) as the Ballerina looking on in horror

which attempted to keep alive the name of Diaghilev's great company is very complicated as they were in a constant state of change. Different managements argued about who had the right to the company name or who had the right to dance a particular ballet. They were, though, great popularizers of ballet, always touring and bringing ballet, almost for the first time, to a mass audience. During this period, the 1930s, the great companies we know today were in their infancy. George Balanchine was making his first choreographic efforts away from the Diaghilev company and playing in small theatres in Europe before moving to America; the Royal Ballet was in the early stages of its development.

Although these young companies were playing to fairly small audiences the seeds were being sown for the great flowering of ballet to-day. As they were small they could take risks when giving opportunities to young dancers and choreographers, and it is from these companies that many modern classic works, such as *Façade* by Frederick Ashton, have come. The larger Ballets Russes companies on the other hand were forced to play more popular ballets in much the same way as companies like the London Festival Ballet or American Ballet Theater do today. They have to spend a great part of their year, to the annoyance of their dancers, performing popular classics such as *Swan Lake* or *The Nutcracker* which almost guarantee full theatres. Full theatres are essential in an age when a large part of the company's income must come from ticket sales.

The Ballet Russe de Monte Carlo had perhaps one great advantage. It discovered the 'baby ballerinas', Baronova, Toumanova and Riabouchinska. At the age of thirteen these three headed the company, guaranteeing endless publicity and, incidentally, at a very young age creating some great roles in the international repertory, in works such as *Beau Danube, Children's Games* and *Graduation Ball.*

They were not alone during this period in having great opportunities when young. At the same time Fonteyn was working with Ashton, and before 1939 had created several major roles including *Les Patineurs* and *Apparitions* and at the age of twenty danced Aurora in *The Sleeping Beauty*. Beryl Grey danced her first Swan Lake at the age of fifteen, *Giselle* at seventeen and *The Sleeping Beauty* at Covent Garden two years later. There has recently been a trend away from giving dancers major opportunities so young with less than happy results. Starting young did not affect the length of the dancing careers of the ballerinas mentioned above. Indeed Margot Fonteyn is still dancing and Toumanova has occasionally appeared in films, most notably in Alfred Hitchcock's *Torn Curtain* in which she 'spots' an escaping spy while doing her famous fouettés! The only notable exception to this trend has been George Balanchine who regularly creates new ballets for very young dancers.

The ever-widening world of dance now offers endless opportunities for the professional dancer, but at the same time more and more people are attracted to a stage career and are able to find places at the many ballet or theatre schools. The result is that dancers usually have to work even harder, and be even more talented, than before in order to be sure of a place in a good company.

Anthony Dowell
Supreme Classical Dancer
4

Anthony Dowell is one of the supreme classical dancers of our time. He can be a sparkling technician in a difficult classical variation or a self-effacing partner presenting his ballerina to the audience. He can be a passionate actor in a great role such as Romeo or cope with the complexities of a modern ballet. He has also been narrator in a ballet, *A Wedding Bouquet* by Frederick Ashton, telling Gertrude Stein's witty story.

Anthony Dowell is now, at thirty-seven, at the peak of a great career which involves travelling regularly between London and New York partnering some of the greatest ballerinas. Until he left the Royal Ballet, his 'home' for so many years, to dance one season with American Ballet Theater he had spent his life in rather a closed world, something not unusual for the young dancer. He had been particularly sheltered as he moved with no particular problems from his first school to the Royal Ballet School and then into the company. He had been further protected from a great deal of outside influence by a close and very happy family life, so happy and, fortunately, so convenient, that he did not become a boarder at the Royal Ballet School. But how did he take his first ballet steps? This is the first question which comes into my mind when I talk to a dancer whether star or corps de ballet member. Perhaps I hope that one day I will get a really unusual answer, but most dancers start so young that often there is no particular reason. Anthony is no exception. 'My sister was taking lessons from June Hampshire, mother of the actress Susan Hampshire. My mother just thought it would be easier for her if we were both at the same place at the same time. She wasn't a ballet mother and didn't push me into dancing as a career. In fact I think that she didn't think of classical dance as a career at all. She probably wanted me to dance like Gene Kelly whom she admired. Now I think I'd like to dance like him, in that wonderful relaxed style!'

This almost accidental introduction to the world of dance is a story I have heard many times from people such as Christopher Gable and Edward Villella, both dancers who helped establish dancing as a career for boys in recent years. But at what point did Anthony get the bug to take dancing up as a career? He is fairly sure of the answer. 'We were very lucky to give our annual performances in a real theatre, the Fortune, right in the centre of London, which is much more magical than a school hall. I think I got hooked onto theatre as a whole not just dancing. That was just one possible way of getting into the theatre

Anthony Dowell
relaxing at home

business, but I was just as keen at designing sets and costumes, making paper figures for my own toy theatre. I still design costumes occasionally and I think an all-round interest in theatre does help your performance. Ballet is such a closed world that it is important to have another interest even if it's still tied up with the theatre. Come to think of it, it almost has to be tied up with the theatre as you have so little time to spend anywhere else!'

The most important factor for any young person setting out on a career in dance is to have a good basic schooling. If you are just attending to pass a Saturday morning it is all too easy to accidentally go to a second rate teacher. In this sense Anthony was lucky as Mrs Hampshire was not only a respected teacher, but also was very helpful with advice and through her conversations with Anthony's parents convinced them that there was a chance he could make a career. After studying with her he entered the Royal Ballet School. Remembering those early years he says 'I didn't like school at all at the start. I wanted to dance all the time and they gave a lot of emphasis to general education. Looking back I realize only too well how sensible they were, but what child likes schoolwork? Now there is even more of it and a very good thing too. I know I have had a good career, but other dancers may have to change career for many different reasons, either by accident or their own choice. It's very good if they have just a little education. I wasn't very good at concentrating at dancing either as it happens. Some things, like turns, came very easily to me which made me a bit lazy. It also made my mind lazy, too. I never analyzed what I was doing which is very bad. You have to understand what you are doing as only that way will you be able to correct any faults. I think I needed very strict teachers to keep me at it and funnily enough the very strict ones, there were a couple I was completely scared of, got the best work out of me. It's not easy to say it, but at that age you really need discipline if you are in the ballet, perhaps more than other occupations. Mistakes made out of carelessness then will ruin any chance of a career.'

When Anthony went to the Upper (Senior) School of the Royal Ballet things improved. 'I worked much better there as I saw students who were much better than me. I started to get an idea of what all this work was being done for. I also saw dancers from the company working which was an inspiration. I think it's so important to watch others to discover your own faults. I also enjoyed classes by Harold Turner, a great dancer in his day who gave wonderful performances in class. It shows how your dancing is slowly leading into the theatre. Also these dancers take an interest in you, one adds to your technical strength with a little hint, another just says something nice to give you confidence. It's up to the student to try and put this jigsaw of millions of little pieces together to make a complete picture. Oddly enough when the picture is more or less complete and you start work, even become a 'star', you are still at school. We carry on doing our daily class with a teacher correcting. We then go on to a rehearsal with a choreographer or ballet master correcting and then we give a performance and the critics correct us. Or try to.'

Once through schooling, what next? Well, for an outstanding student at the Royal Ballet School the aim is to join the company. Anthony was not particularly worried about joining the company: 'I just accepted that at that time you could expect to work for a time in the Opera Ballet so I went there for one year taking part in operas such as *Aïda*. For me it was just a question of which of the two Royal Ballet companies I would join. I wanted to join the main company at Covent Garden very badly. As it turned out I got what I wanted and really was thrown in at the deep end as we went straight off on tour to Russia.'

If early days in the main company presented some problems, it still must have seemed very exciting compared to the routine work of the Opera Ballet. 'Not really' says Anthony 'if you are in the corps de ballet you have much the same problem. In fact having to stand around like human scenery or be animated guests at a ball can serve a useful function in a dancer's training. I don't think it did me any harm as when I dance one of the classics such as *Swan Lake* or *Sleeping Beauty* I have to stand and watch the corps de ballet dancing or have to graciously receive presents from my courtiers.

34

Anthony Dowell
rehearsing with Merle
Park

Coping with these parts is almost as difficult as the
dancing as you have to look completely natural on
the stage.'

Once in the company there are always personal
problems of adjusting and becoming a member of a
group. Anthony's personal background meant that
he was not the most outgoing person and he had some
difficulties, but he soon got to know people, if only
because of the tour to Russia which meant that they
spent so much time cooped up together. He enjoyed
the corps de ballet work and looks back on it
wistfully. 'We didn't seem to take it *that* seriously
even though we worked hard and gave, I hope, good
performances. We just got to the theatre on time, did
what we had to do, changed costumes endlessly in the
big ballets, tried not to look too bored, ate huge meals
whenever we liked, and then went home. I wish I
could do that now, in fact I wonder how I did it then. I
remember wondering what happened if the principal
dancers ever had headaches and didn't feel like going
on. Now I know only too well. If only you could
combine that lovely relaxed approach with work as a

35

principal. It would be much easier on the nerves.'

All dancers are waiting for the breakthrough, the role which will make them noticed and let both audiences and company know that they are just a little 'special'. Anthony was first noticed by a large public at Covent Garden dancing a solo in *Napoli*. 'I learned a lot from Erik Bruhn who arranged this ballet. I admired his style—I suppose I see myself as the same type of dancer. By this time Nureyev had joined the company following his escape from Russia. I was too low in the company to feel any challenge and could only learn from him. He was the most stimulating influence.'

Learning from other dancers, the process of continual schooling, is essential for any young dancer. But it can also have pitfalls. 'It's very important' comments Anthony, 'that you know *how* to learn from other dancers. It really is learning and not copying. You must watch the way they work and try to apply some things to yourself, but it must come out looking like *you* dancing and not a copy of your model. If you try to force yourself to turn like one dancer or jump like another it can have serious consequences. You can harm your body as well as harming your own personality. Copying gestures is even worse!'

The young dancer slowly works his or her way up the company. As technique and stage presence improve better roles will come their way and they may find that they have a certain talent for a particular type of role, the classical cavalier or the demi-caractère part. They will have to be open to many different influences as it can be fatal to specialize too soon. 'Oddly enough,' says Anthony, 'my earliest interest was in one act ballets. This probably dates back to the early ballet performances I saw. I preferred a whole new story and scene each act to the full-length ballets. Those I did see, such as *Coppélia*, I didn't particularly like and certainly had no urge to dance them. When I joined the company I had no pre-conceived ideas and I can't think of anything in particular I wanted to dance. Now I suppose people think of me first as a classical Prince, though of course I have danced many other character and modern ballets, and its odd to think that this was in no way planned. Perhaps this is what often makes dance such an adventurous and dangerous career for the young dancer. There you are, very young, having been fairly cut off from much of everyday life, without the advice of agents of managers which a young actor might have. You have the help perhaps of your family or a few close friends, though they can often be too heavily involved in the business. You have to judge for yourself in the end. Perhaps that's why dancers never seem happy. They are either dancing too much or not enough, when in reality what they are doing is probably just right. I know I was not worried until roles were almost pushed in front of me. First dancing in revivals and then, the big breakthrough, having a ballet created for me.'

Being spotted by a choreographer, any choreographer let alone one as great as Frederick Ashton or Antony Tudor, is what every dancer dreams of. However much satisfaction is coming from dancing big roles in classical ballets or exciting character parts, it is not the same as having a role specially created for you. Most choreographers today really work with the dancer and do not just use them as mechanical dancing bodies. They encourage the dancer to take part by suggesting steps and movements. There are so many famous stories, told many times, of dancers arriving late for rehearsals, falling over or tripping up and the mistake being kept in the ballet. Anthony recalls 'When we were working on *The Dream* with Frederick Ashton, by we I mean Antoinette Sibley and myself, we were not even sure at the start that we would be dancing the principal roles. We thought we would be two of the lovers. It was nerve-racking wondering if we were the type, or dancing well enough for Sir Fred. It was like a long audition. As it turned out he was planning to use us. He works in a very intuitive way. He suggests a mood and asks you to do something. I remember him once saying he visualized a fountain (this was later) and asked us to do something. We did, and he loved it. Then you have the difficult problem of going back to square one and trying to think what it was you actually did! Other choreographers work in different ways. Kenneth MacMillan shows you the steps he

Anthony Dowell as Nijinsky with Rudolf Nureyev as Valentino dancing a Tango in the film *Valentino*

imagines and you work on polishing them. Hans van Manen has everything very planned and you go through the same polishing process. Antony Tudor, who made *Shadowplay* for me, was very different, a really rather hard process. He didn't explain what he wanted at all. I just had to try to move in a way which expressed what he wanted, though I may not have been sure. It's difficult to describe. You just have to trust the choreographer and hope he has a complete conception in his head. The dancer does have a great responsibility here; to judge the mood correctly and not introduce anything extra into a role, especially in performance, after the choreographer has set it.'

38

Dancers never work in isolation, even for a short solo. There will be a choreographer or teacher to correct them. A moment's rehearsal alone is still reflected in the ever-present mirror. If you are in the corps de ballet you must learn to work as part of a group. If you are a principal dancing an international repertoire you must know how to adjust to suit many partners. You may also have a special relationship with one partner. Of Antoinette Sibley, Anthony remembers their early meetings. 'Working together was always a happy experience. You have to be totally committed to each other and we found that easy. We always seemed to be in sympathy over whatever we were working on. When we worked on *The Dream* I thought that all partnerships must be as easy. Antoinette had already danced with other principals of the company and I assumed it was the same for her each time. She says this wasn't the case so I am happy to take her word for it. It also worked for the purely practical reason that we were physically right for each other, the right height and proportions. This alone won't produce a partnership, but there's little hope of one no matter how sympathetic you are to each other if you look odd together!'

Such a wonderful relationship can produce some problems. When the audience sees such a perfect partnership they naturally want more of the same. A true artist will not be happy continually doing the same thing and will want any partnership to develop. Anthony did dance with many other ballerinas and says that each time it was a case of starting each time afresh, working out a good relationship. Sadly his partnership with Antoinette eventually came to an end when after a series of accidents and illness she decided to retire to a happy married life.

Up to this time Anthony's career had been a continuous line, from first steps to the stage of the Royal Opera House at Covent Garden. He had of course made various guest performances, but not as many as you might have expected for a dancer of his stature. He was very much at home with the Royal Ballet. He had become very popular in America through the many tours the Royal Ballet made there and had partnered some of the world's greatest ballerinas when they made guest appearances in England. He finally decided to make a break and dance for one year with American Ballet Theater in New York. His decision was headline news in the dance world in Britain with stories of arguments and disputes, all untrue. People felt that there had to be a dramatic reason for his decision to go, but in reality it was just that Anthony felt he had to get some new experience, possibly being a little too set in his ways.

Dancing in America gave him a greater range and presented new challenges. 'It really is starting out all over again even for someone as established as me,' says Anthony, 'perhaps arriving with a reputation makes it even more difficult. If you were joining the corps de ballet you would, I think, make friends easier. I was not completely happy, but I was doing it for the work not the social life.' As it turned out the year away, and now his regular commuting between American Ballet Theater and the Royal Ballet, have given him greater authority as a dancer. He has also been able to work more with Natalia Makarova, most recently on her new production of *La Bayadère*. Rehearsing this production presented problems he first encountered when he started dancing in a company. 'I was dancing the role of Solor, the Prince who descends to the Kingdom of the Shades looking for his love, Nikiya', says Anthony. 'It's a big classical role, but rehearsing it is the same for me as for the corps de ballet. If something is being created, inevitably things do not fall into place first time. We all get a bit bored waiting while pieces are revised or gone over for the umpteenth time. Such a big production also takes a long long time to rehearse and by the time we principals come together with the corps de ballet we can almost hear them thinking what a terrible bore the whole thing is. And then you do a solo, determined to show what you can do and the whole thing starts to come to life. Makarova is such a hard worker, when she shows the corps de ballet a step and then does her own solos they really appreciate it. Looking back I think one of the nicest things is when you do have some effect on your fellow dancers. When the corps de ballet applaud your first solo when you are a new member of the company it's almost as satisfying as when an audience cheer when

40

the curtain comes down. You know that it's a unique
occasion for the audience, but the dancers have sat
round for days on end watching you rehearse.'

It is hard to resist asking a dancer such as Anthony
Dowell what his advice to a young dancer is. He says,

Anthony Dowell in
Frederick Ashton's
Daphnis and Chloé

41

'A while back I remember saying that I wouldn't advise anyone to take this business up, which isn't very helpful'. It may not be helpful but it reflects truly how hard dancers consider their profession to be. All artists think they are the hardest working, singers or actors alike, but perhaps dancing takes the greatest dedication when very young and is also the most time consuming. From an early age you devote your life to a very full daily round which will eventually lead to a day which may begin with class early in the morning, continue through rehearsals which go on endlessly, to a performance which might end quite late. It leaves little time for a private life, and little energy for much socializing after the performance. A dancer like Anthony can count on some help with the business side of life, the buying of plane tickets, the booking of hotels, the arrangement of performance and rehearsal dates. Somehow he must keep himself fit and in perfect form the whole time, never forgetting that wherever he is there will be a class to do. On top of this there is inevitably some nervous strain before a performance. The casual attitude he spoke of when young would be taking too great a risk. He must think about performances, even roles he may be doing sometime in the future. He says, 'I do get nervous in the period before a performance. Not just in the theatre just before curtain up. It's more thinking about the role as a whole for a build-up period.' There are demands on the time of a dancer such as Anthony for charity performances, publicity which might include early morning talk shows, personal appearances, all the razzmattazz of show-business which now accompanies the incredible growth of interest in ballet. Anthony is not exaggerating when he says, perhaps not too seriously, 'There are almost too many things in your life apart from dancing, not least of all interviews like this!' Coping with it all and still being able to be a wonderful example of a complete dancer is a measure of Anthony's talent. He may hesitate to offer too much advice to a young dancer, but perhaps without knowing it his perfect polished performances are in themselves a textbook for every young dancer to take note of.

Training for Ballet

5

The dancer has a short working life with only the greatest having a dancing career lasting much after the age of forty. Many, of course, continue to perform in character roles or behind the scenes as teachers and ballet masters, but the years of training are not aimed at that. Ending the career early is balanced by starting early. So early, in fact, that the decision will have had to be made very much younger than most readers of this book will be: Most dancers expect to be on the stage and earning by the age of eighteen, or even earlier, and some of the great dancers who have tackled very big roles in their teens were mentioned at the end of the last chapter.

Lessons can start as early as four or five if you really want to dance. For a girl it is more important to start training early, providing that the training is controlled, serious and in no way forces the dancer to be a performer too soon. It is particularly harmful to start point work too early. Every young girl wants to stand on her toes as soon as she starts dancing and it is very difficult for a good teacher to devise a satisfying programme which only introduces point work gradually when the soft bones of the feet have hardened and begun to be capable of bearing the body's weight. For boys the problem is not so serious and any reasonably athletic boy who wants to dance can take it up as late as about fourteen. The later he leaves it, of course, the less chance there is of him becoming a star performer, but he could still make a good career, particularly in modern dance.

Dance Schools
Unfortunately keenness, and even ability, may not be

the most important thing in deciding to become a professional dancer. If the aim is to become a classical dancer the choice of a good teacher in the early years is vital. A teacher must be able to achieve the high standards demanded for entry into schools like the Royal Ballet School in London or the School of American Ballet in New York. If your aim is to join one of the major national companies, attendance at one of the national schools is almost essential. If you do not get into one your career is not ruined as there are many excellent private schools in all countries, but it will mean adjusting your ideas about where you will work. Major companies do, of course, take in dancers from outside their own schools, but they tend to do so at soloist or principal level, in other words dancers who have already established themselves elsewhere.

Left: Schoolwork happens alongside ballet at the Royal Ballet School in London

The number of young dancers who get into any of the major schools is very small, perhaps only twenty or thirty each year out of hundreds of applicants. The standards of entry to the Junior Royal Ballet School, known as White Lodge, are much the same as those applying to other schools of a similar standard. Considerable dancing ability is almost taken for granted and often representatives of the school visit smaller schools of all types in advance to scout for available talent. Nowadays auditions are much more thorough than they were and extensive medical examinations are made, not only to make sure that the prospective dancer is healthy and able to stand up to the rigorous training, but also to see if they are

Opposite: Young girls at the barre, a scene typical of ballet schools the world over

45

the right proportions for dancing and conform to the image of the school. When you read about these tests or see them in films such as *The Children Of Theatre Street*, which shows daily life at the Kirov School, you might think back to small, unattractive La Camargo and the 'little hunchback' Taglioni, who might not have reached the standards demanded today. Of course, this emphasis on physical type has advantages. If there are limited places it is sensible to give them to those most likely to succeed and most likely to fit into the ensemble, but it does make it harder for unusual talent to emerge. The emphasis on physical perfection may be at the expense of dramatic talent. Marie Sallé made her impact through expression not technique, and so did Margot Fonteyn.

Perhaps the Royal Ballet of today would not accept her on account of her feet when she was young; Ashton described them as little pats of butter.

The regime in a ballet school is invariably highly disciplined. Dance students have to be particularly dedicated as they must cope with the rigour of the daily ballet classes as well as general education. This is a fairly recent development, which has the advantage of giving the dancer a good educational base if the career should be cut short through lack of talent or physical injury. The Royal Danish School has particularly close links with the Royal Danish Ballet and more than any other school seems part of the same family—and often is, as there is a high incidence there of children following in parent's

After the barre a moment of tiredness or frustration for the young star Nadezhda Pavlova of the Bolshoi Ballet

footsteps. Students in Denmark also have the added strain, although they would not think of it as that, of appearing in many ballets in the repertoire.

Daily life is remarkably similar in all the schools. Of course, there are small differences: the Kirov School looks rather spartan, the School of American Ballet has an air of showbiz, but the round of dance classes is much the same. At a residential school the pupils get up early and may take their first ballet class at 8:30, followed by a series of academic lessons usually leaning a little towards theatrical and musical studies, but including a variety of basic studies from mathematics to literature. Just as in a normal school the pupils have homework, but they will also have a second ballet class, perhaps concentrating on one aspect of the course. In Denmark the younger boys and girls, aged from around five to eleven, take classes together, but will then work separately as in most schools. The girls will work on line, grace, elegance (as well as the usual technical grind and then pointwork) while the boys will develop virtuosity and strength. They will only come together after a term or two, depending on their age, to work on partnering essential for the pas de deux, as well as corps de ballet work. The complexities and techniques of lifting the ballerina with no apparent effort will take years of work.

In Denmark the progression from school to company is continuous, as with the Kirov. The Royal

Young boys in the spacious studio of the school of the Royal Swedish Ballet in Stockholm. Reflected in the mirror is their teacher Charles Mudry who has been influential in the increasing importance of Swedish male dancers in ballet today

Ballet School is divided into the Upper and Lower Schools which means that around the age of fifteen or sixteen there is a break, with the best pupils going into the Upper school which has closer links with the company and shares studios with them. The School of American Ballet is a special case as it is non-residential and does not offer academic studies.

From School to Stage

Although all these large schools, and the Paris Opéra school which is enormous should not be forgotten, are closely linked with companies, they are not there for the sole purpose of providing dancers for these companies. In practice, having trained a large number of good dancers they can usually only offer places to one or two of them. The competition, whether in Leningrad or London, is intense. Graduates of the Leningrad School may well return to the provincial companies where they started out, which certainly helps to improve the standards of these companies. Graduates of the Royal Ballet School may find their way into one of the other, very few, English companies although they are more likely to look for work in Europe. There are few companies, large or small, which do not have English dancers. In recent years graduates of the School of American Ballet have also been trying to find work in Europe, particularly as Balanchine has had so much influence in Germany and Switzerland. The formation of the Common Market made the movement of dancers (except Americans who still need a work permit) much easier, though in the past there had been few problems as dancers were in demand. Every small opera house in Germany—and there are over twenty major ones—has a ballet company, mostly to dance in the operas or operettas, and their schools simply could not provide enough dancers.

Most dancers naturally aim to get into the main national company, for only by aiming for the top can they hope to achieve even a measure of success. The study of ballet does not allow for compromise, particularly in the case of ballerinas. A competent boy, who is a good partner though perhaps a little unexciting in his solo dancing, can still be guaranteed a fair living in Europe and America, though

Ballerinas of the New York City Ballet, who seem to start work and appear in leading roles much younger than any others, seen from the wings of the Royal Opera House, Covent Garden

away from the main centres. A ballerina on the other hand has to fight for everything and work for everything, simply because so many girls take up ballet.

Work in one of the small companies is naturally not as satisfying as the opportunity to work with a major national company and with some of the great choreographers (perhaps alongside some of the greatest stars). Many of these small companies, however, can perform works by the modern masters or by young choreographers working in the modern classical style. Frustrations though, may arise over the limited number of performances devoted to ballet alone, compared to the dozens spent waltzing in operas or dancing in operettas, or even worse, simply standing around in ballroom scenes as human scenery.

Another drawback of this type of work is the long-term insecurity. Contracts in the German opera houses, for instance, are usually given for one year at a time and although you can usually be sure of renewing your contract if you have worked well, sometimes the decision is taken out of your hands by a change of director in the theatre. This happens quite often in opera houses and new directors tend to bring in new people. Of course this may not happen, but dancers have to be prepared to be mobile and keep an ear open for news of vacancies in other companies. Or

they can go on the audition trail across Europe at the beginning of each year when companies are hiring dancers for the following season which usually starts in September. This is another good reason why dancers are referred to as 'gypsies'!

While at the ballet school, studying classical ballet, it is highly likely that a student will learn tap-dancing, jazz-dancing and modern dancing, all of which will be useful for careers away from the big companies. A well-trained classical dancer can very easily adapt to modern dance and many of the most famous modern dancers today were trained in the classical school. Training in all aspects of dance is now essential as even a great classical company like the Royal Ballet will have modern dances in its repertoire and dancers may have to change during one programme from the style of Glen Tetley, for example, to that of Ashton. They may well have to tap or dance in high heels. Classical ballet is no longer a closed world.

Dancers of the Royal Ballet such as Lesley Collier now dance a classical ballet one evening and then may have to change to a completely modern ballet such as *Dances of Albion* by Glen Tetley on another

6 Patrick Hinson
At the New York City Ballet

'I'm twenty. Isn't that old!'

Well, I certainly didn't think so, but coming from Patrick Hinson, a member of the corps de ballet of the New York City Ballet, it made me realize what a young business ballet is, and also how competitive. Not only do dancers start young, hope to make a name for themselves young, they also end their careers relatively early. At each stage the dancer has to face problems of training and cope with adult work problems much earlier than people in other professions, in the arts or outside.

'I was a relatively late starter' says Patrick, 'I only started tap lessons at six! This was at my regular academic school in Blanchester, Ohio. As you can guess this small town, not far from Cincinatti, isn't exactly an artistic centre, but the school had, for the time, an adventurous policy and introduced dance classes. They were optional and started with tap so we all joined in. It was fun rather than learning and suits boys as well as girls. After a year of this I decided I quite liked it and wanted to carry on the next year with ballet. This was when the class got a bit smaller as most of the other boys dropped out. Soon I was the only one left. It didn't worry me at all, none of the others minded particularly. There weren't any problems. At least if there were any problems, let's say I wasn't aware of them. Of course I was still doing my academic lessons and sport as well. Funnily enough doing my dancing didn't make me careful in sports, afraid to hurt a leg or something. I remember being the one who took the most risks. Dancing seemed as natural as sport. I wasn't doing any long-term planning. I just danced for the hell of it!'

This natural enthusiasm is important in the early stages of most dancers' lives. You have to have it otherwise you soon get tired of the regular classes and disciplined work. Usually enthusiasm is backed up by a keen parent and ballet has an unusually high proportion of them. Ballet mothers have become

Patrick Hinson rehearsing in the studios of the School of American Ballet

almost as famous as their offspring, constantly backstage ready with advice, fruit juice and newly-darned point shoes. Patrick's mother fortunately did not come into this category, though she had had some experience in the arts. 'She had been to an art school when she was young', Patrick remembers, 'and I know she had been friendly with Joel Grey, the wonderful performer who was the M.C. in both film and stage versions of *Cabaret*. She encouraged me, but without any pressure. At first my father just went along with it, but after my parents separated he really was a great help. In fact he did a lot more than just encourage me as he had the bother in later years of getting me to and from the dance school I went to in Cincinatti at the University Dance Department. Without his practical help it would have been impossible for me to get the sort of training necessary when young.'

Most young children are natural performers and love being on stage at school or for charity shows. Patrick was no exception. 'I really wanted to be out there doing it. I don't really know why, but it could have something to do with me being the middle child of a family of seven. This may sound a bit serious and of course I didn't know it at the time but being up there in the spotlight, my, there's no better way of getting attention. I also never had any nerves, but perhaps most children are like that. It's when you get older you discover them as you are aware of the responsibility, even in the back line of the corps.'

'I was OK at academic studies at school, but more and more of my time was taken up with dancing. Having to commute to Cincinatti meant missing classes which wasn't very popular at the school. Anyway they encouraged me to take up dancing seriously so I more or less moved right over to the University, which had an important dance department. One of my earliest and strongest memories was of being able to watch Alicia Markova teaching. After my own class I'd creep in and watch her's. She'd demonstrate style wonderfully while sitting. Even now when I see photographs of her in a sitting pose I think of her beautiful ports de bras, how she could convey style with simple gestures, rather than her dancing. In some ways I see the same thing now with

54

Mr Balanchine. He can demonstrate steps of course, in that way he's phenomenal, but the real magic is in style conveyed through a simple gesture.'

All this training, as every student and parent will know across the world, takes a lot of money. Parents often have to be rich or prepared to make considerable sacrifices to pay for schooling which very often does not qualify for state or city aid. Patrick's parents were comfortably off, but not rich. 'It was such a help when the university offered me small amounts to take part in performances as they helped pay for the education. By the time I was ten I had taken part in big productions, particularly the annual *Nutcracker* when I danced the little Nutcracker Prince in a version where a cavalier partners the Sugar Plum Fairy in the pas des deux. This was wonderful experience as no matter how hard you work in class and rehearsal you feel that the stage is the place you want to be. Also doing productions like this you can, in a sense, make your mistakes and try out different make-up, different hair-styles. Presentation is important, but once you are in a company you don't have all that much opportunity to experiment. These performances were invaluable experience in every way. You learn how to cope with problems without awkwardness, how to cope with the unexpected. Also how to go onto the stage at short notice and give a performance. I remember taking over a role in a modern ballet by James Truitte—it seemed the most natural thing to do and as I have already said I never suffered from nerves at all. Perhaps it was just innocence and not knowing how awful things can turn out, but also I found technique fairly easy.'

The daily class to perfect individual technique is only one aspect of training, as Patrick says, 'We soon started to have lessons in double work which is equally essential for the corps de ballet as for the principals. You spend a lot of time just holding ballerinas up! We also learned jazz dancing, though in my case not so much, and an amount of modern dance which is fairly important these days when companies employ such a wide range of choreographers. I don't know why, but I did seem to concentrate on the classical side. Possibly this was

The New York City Ballet's famous director George Balanchine

because I was the only boy for quite a time and spent a fair bit of time preparing for classical performances.'

By this time Patrick was aware of dance in the world outside, largely through film and television. He is one of a whole generation of young dancers who started training long after Rudolf Nureyev had left Russia for the West and had had such a dramatic effect on the standard of male dancing generally. The possibility of dance as a career, even a profitable career, for a boy had been well established. Patrick had grown up in the fairly confined world of Cincinatti, seeing only the occasional guest brought in for the bigger performances. It was almost taken for granted that he would join the Cincinatti company. He remembers, 'I was still doing academic work, but dance training was the main thing and dance was sure to be my career. I had opportunities to dance and a contract was sure. We even had good people coming to do productions, including Frederick Franklin. He was very helpful and largely through his advice, or at least the possibilities he showed me, my mind slowly turned to the outside world. I hadn't given serious thought to New York and the larger companies then, but gradually I realised

Patrick Hinson as the Bluebird in *The Sleeping Beauty*, a Cincinatti ballet production

that it would be foolish to limit my horizons and settle for the obvious where I was.'

Competition to get into the School of American Ballet or the American Ballet Theater School is intense. In the case of SAB many places are taken almost by invitation. Representatives talent spot across America offering places to talent they think outstanding. Patrick did not find things too difficult, if for slightly amusing reasons. 'I just went to New York and walked right into SAB and asked for an interview and audition. Oddly enough they said yes and I did one. Then I asked them for the cash to pay for my studies, which I think surprised them a bit. They must have asked themselves who this kid with big ideas was. It really didn't take that much nerve as I was trying for a place knowing that if they said no I could go right back to Cincinatti and take up my contract there! As they didn't immediately come up with an offer I felt I could accept, I went right over to ABT School and more or less did the same thing there. They seemed to like me and offered me a place in their summer school with the possibility of getting into their 'junior' company. This appealed to me as you don't get such an offer in New York every day. Kids are killing themselves in class to do it. This I soon found out when I attended the classes. The competition and the atmosphere was incredible, not to mention the numbers. It put me off the whole idea. It really upset me to see all this fighting for work. So back to Cincinatti I went.'

Coping with this type of situation is exactly the sort of problem a teenager in another field would not have to do. There is not only the strain of the very physical work which leaves you drained after doing two classes a day, but also the emotional pressure. In any case things turned out all right for Patrick as SAB did come up with an offer and he was able to attend the school. The immediate problem was to get out of the Cincinatti contract without offending anyone. He had to make the decision to leave the school he had been attending for the best part of ten years and which had given him the self-confidence for his New York auditions. But in ballet you cannot afford to lose a year. A place in a school or a contract with a company will not be there next year and you know only too well how many other, even younger, dancers are waiting to snap them up. Next year is too late. You might even have reached the ripe old age of eighteen by then!

With a solid course of training behind him, and the polish of classes by such eminent teachers as Stanley Williams, Patrick was soon offered a place in George Balanchine's New York City Ballet, in the corps de ballet, where he still is after two years. Patrick says quite naturally, 'Of course I think that by now I should have done more, but probably so does every member of the corps de ballet or every principal. We are all too keen. Even if you have a roster of good roles you still watch others and think "why aren't I doing that". There is always the frustration of watching others do what you feel you could do, perhaps better. All dancers have to think like this. It's not that we are conceited, it's just that we work continually to make ourselves better and have to believe in ourselves.'

A corps de ballet dancer has the problem of knowing what work to do on his or her own initiative. You will have the roles you are given to rehearse according to the schedule worked out by the ballet master, but if you are keen it is very wise to work on some roles yourself, possibly roles for which you are tenth cast! It is as well to be ready, just in case. . . .

Patrick was justifiably pleased when his name went up on the company board as one of those chosen to work with Jerome Robbins on his famous ballet for three sailors on leave, *Fancy Free*. It was also the basis of a wonderful musical film, *On the Town*. 'You are keen to learn the steps, but you do not really know whether you will be dancing the role or not. You have to be able to work alongside, or more often behind, an army of others. You have to work as though *you* are sure you're going to be performing it. You have to keep yourself on peak form just in case, as the rehearsals may stretch over several weeks. At times you feel that it isn't worth it and those are the difficult times. You may have a depression and convince yourself that Mr Robbins is never going to use you. Then the moment you let up in rehearsal or don't attend that's the moment he wants you. As it happened I didn't get to dance it, but now I know it so

who knows what will happen in the future. In any case you have to take whatever chances there are to work with such a great choreographer. You still get something out of it even if it isn't a performance. On the other hand I have gone on with a minimum rehearsal in both *Napoli* and *Theme and Variations*. Someone's ill and you are next in line. If you have kept your eyes open you will have done some work on the role just in case. If not you have a busy few hours before the show! It's at times like that that training and experience count. It helps if you can throw off triple turns or good jumps with confidence, but at times like these it's more important to know the steps, do single turns in time with the others and hold your ballerina up straight. The tricks have to wait till you've made some sort of name for yourself and can hope to do the occasional guest performance of a classical pas de deux. The best I've done so far is to go back to Cincinatti to dance Bluebird in their *Sleeping Beauty*.'

Balancing all these different problems at work can be difficult in a big company where there is not

The original cast of Jerome Robbins's *Fancy Free*, the story of three sailors on leave for the first time in New York. (Robbins is leaning on the bar.) This ballet was the inspiration for the film *On the Town*

constant personal attention. There is coaching from great figures such as Balanchine himself, classes from good teachers, but after that a dancer has to look after himself. You are also living in a big city where finding an apartment may not be easy, especially on a dancer's salary. Though the theatre union, Equity, has improved pay considerably in both Britain and America, corps de ballet members are not so well off. In America there is the additional problem that some dancer's have 'lay-off' periods when they are not working and sign on to collect unemployment pay.

One of the attractions of ballet life for some at least is the chance to tour. Patrick has mixed feelings, 'I've not been in the company very long but already we have toured to Britain, Denmark, Germany and France. I'm still not sure whether I like it or not. The advantages are obvious and for me have been mostly connected with ballet. In Copenhagen for instance it was wonderful to take classes with the Royal Danish Ballet. Perhaps I'll get used to it in time, but I find it very difficult to balance the work which takes up a lot of the day and most evenings, with getting the most out of the city I'm visiting. I suppose it does widen your knowledge if you take every opportunity to see things, other companies, galleries or just the sights.'

At this stage in a dancer's career it is difficult to predict what might happen next. New York City Ballet offers wonderful opportunities, but you cannot ignore what is happening elsewhere. It is possible that a different repertoire might attract Patrick at some time, just as it is that possible Balanchine might include him in a new ballet, always the most exciting part of New York City Ballet life. As Patrick says, 'You just have got to stick at it, work hard for yourself so that you know the value of your own work and be ready for that opportunity when it comes.'

Modern Dance

7

Nowadays it is possible to study modern dance in the same way as classical ballet. The modern dance schools in general, however, do not provide a complete education in the manner of many of the larger residential, classically based schools. They offer instead courses that vary from the occasional weekly lesson for a dancer to add to his or her existing range to a complete course designed to prepare the dancer for the stage.

Modern dance has its earliest roots in educational theories of rhythm and movement and not in performances. It was concerned as much with the effect on the individual who studied and how it helped general development as with showing off a technique to an audience. Some of this idea is still alive today, particularly in courses related to the Laban School of dance, partly because it is much easier to take part in modern dance. You need not be a polished theatrical performer capable of the more exciting moves or of sustaining a complex role, to join in, something which is impossible in the classical ballet. This may partly explain why many young people, particularly university students or those more interested in dramatic theatre, feel that they can identify with modern dance. Classical ballet is remote, something to be admired from a distance, firmly on a proscenium stage, that is, one with an arch and usually a curtain. Many performances of modern dance take place in theatres-in-the-round, where the audience sits all round the stage area, or in more informal places, such as school halls or even open spaces like parks and streets.

The style of modern dance is also, literally, more

down to earth and in some ways was a deliberate break away from the restricted world of the classical ballet. The earliest performers at the beginning of this century felt that the dance should relate to real life and be concerned with the issues of the day. Amongst Isadora Duncan's most famous dances was one concerned with the Russian Revolution. They also felt that the dance should be related to the ground and take its inspiration from nature. Martha Graham in particular wanted to use the ground, falling to it and dancing with bare feet on it, rather than aim for the airy flights of classical ballet. In every way these early performers were absolutely against all the ideas of the classical ballet: its artificiality, its fairy-tale themes and its association with the upper classes. Fortunately now that they themselves are well established and modern dance is accepted, both dance forms are coming together and you will find Martha Graham or Glen Tetley using what would be regarded as classical steps, while on old classical company such as the Royal Danish Ballet will perform beautifully a work such as *Aureole* by Paul Taylor, one of Martha Graham's pupils.

Isadora Duncan attempted to form several schools, including one in Moscow at the invitation of the Soviet government, during her stormy career. None of them lasted, either because of shortages of practical necessities such as money and facilities or, most probably, because her style of dance had no real form. She created it from her own natural urge to dance and from her impetuous personality and it would take someone of equal ability and character to recreate the works, they simply cannot be taught to classes of children. Her influence on dance has instead come down to us through performers who saw her and were impressed. After her visit to Russia in 1904, for example, she left a great impression on Mikhail Fokine, who was to become Diaghilev's great choreographer, and the dancer Tamara Karsavina. Isadora would influence the great Russian director and teacher in the dramatic theatre, Stanislavksy, during the revolutionary years.

The first great modern school was formed by Ruth St Denis and Ted Shawn in 1915. Denishawn, as the

Isadora Duncan, heavily draped, in a very typical pose

school was known, taught all forms of dance ranging from Oriental to German Modern. Ruth St Denis had been a famous dancer in Europe as well as America, performing oriental solos based on temple dances. Her most famous role was as an Egyptian dancer, which was inspired by an advertisement for Egyptian Deity cigarettes featuring a large painting of a very exotic looking lady. In its early years the school did not have one recognizable style and it would be up to its most famous pupils to develop their own. Martha Graham is now the best-known, though there were many others who have been influential in forming modern dance, such as Doris Humphrey and Charles Weidman.

Although several of the Denishawn dancers made important contributions, to dancing theory as well as forming companies and schools, it is the Graham technique which is the most famous, and it is now widely used by schools around the world. The school which was formed in London and from which the London Contemporary Dance Theatre grew is based on her technique and her influence is apparent in companies such as the Ballet Rambert.

Martha Graham

Graham was a pupil, then a teacher and company member of the Denishawn School, but by 1923 she was unhappy with the style of dancing and left to start work on her own ideas. Her first recitals still showed the influence of the school in the oriental solos she created for herself, but it was not long before she started on the road which would lead to the discovery of her own technique. She formed a school and from this grew the group which, with great difficulty, she managed to keep together. The company still exists, dancing only her works, although she no longer dances. Her stage presence was particularly strong and people who saw her create a role are never completely satisfied when they see it danced by someone else. However as her roles were based on a firm technique they can still exist. They did not totally depend on her personality as was the case with Isadora.

The school she created still thrives and is a mecca for visiting dancers and teachers to New York. It provides the student with a complete course in the Graham technique and is highly regarded. The other modern dance schools, in New York in particular, are not so well established and are often only schools in the sense that they provide a daily class, not a complete dance education. There are of course notable exceptions, particularly in the case of Merce Cunningham, but, nonetheless, these schools appear to produce the best results from mature dancers who already have some experience, and they are not really suitable for the young dancer just setting out on a career. There is also an additional danger working in one modern dance school for it does not prepare the dancer for all sorts of work, in contrast to most classical or theatrical schools.

Modern Dance Training

America differs from the rest of the world in offering many dance courses at universities. Dance can be taken as one of a mixture of subjects and on an equal footing with them. At the end of the course an

academic degree is awarded. The true value of this system has yet to be realized as far too often dance is taken as a subject just to pass the time or because no other is available. The courses are organized very often by eminent dancers and teachers, but the result is rarely a career on the stage. Many of these universities arrange performances once or twice a year, and one or two have even given rise to full-scale companies, such as in Pittsburgh. The principal dancers usually have full-time, professional contracts with the college, and the students make up the rest of the company as soloists or corps de ballet. It is undoubtedly a good way of giving opportunities to students who cannot afford to go to New York to study, but the vast numbers of people now involved mean that out of the thousands who are working at these college courses, not more than one or two can hope to work in the more professional atmosphere of

Martha Graham created many very dramatic roles based on Biblical and mythical figures. Here she appears as Judith

Avigail Ben Ari of the British Extemporary Dance Company during a class. Floor work at the beginning replaces the barre exercises of classical ballet; both relieve the dancer of the need to concentrate entirely on balance which will come later in the class

the School of American Ballet, and eventually the New York City Ballet or the American Ballet Theater.

These universities often invite a professional group to be a company in residence, which is a useful way of providing funds for some of the excellent small modern dance companies which often find it difficult to stay together for a whole year. The dancers will give classes, coach individual dancers in roles and also give performances at the university theatre for perhaps one term. For this all their expenses will be paid and they will have the much-needed time to work on new projects, something they could not do in the harsh, commercial world outside. This contact with professional dancers is essential for the stud-

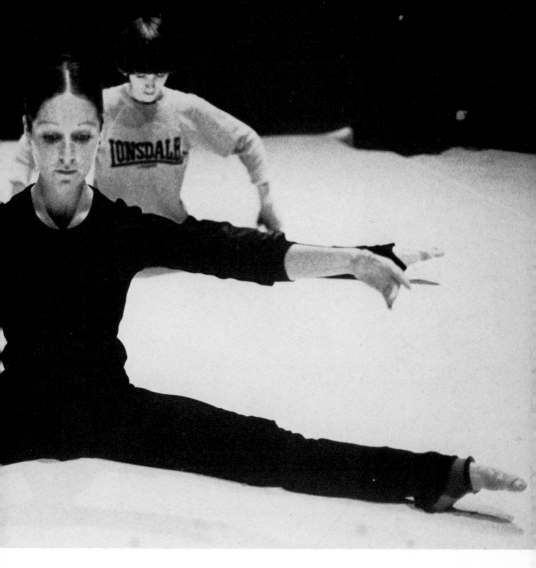

ents and often much more important than their regular teaching if they, too, hope to make the stage their career. It is also a good warning about the difficulties of such a career when they see people of excellent reputation whom they have admired on stage, finding it difficult to keep the group together for lack of money.

There are few courses like this available outside America. Canadian universities have taken up the idea, and there are two courses of this type in Britain. The first is a three-year, full-time course for a Bachelor of Arts degree at the Laban Centre for Movement and Dance which is part of Goldsmiths' College of the University of London. The course covers dance and many subjects related to it:

A modern dance performance by students of the Rambert Academy

anatomy, choreography, dance history, notation and music.

The other course is the result of an idea by the enterprising Ballet Rambert. This small company was started in the 1920s by Marie Rambert. For years it was a classical company dancing an excellent repertoire of important works, particularly those of Antony Tudor, but the financial problems of touring forced the company to change its policy in 1963. Overnight it became a modern dance company, smaller, more compact and much more economical to run; no great sets had to be transported around the country and no longer was a full-scale orchestra needed. Since that time it has grown into one of the most important modern companies and has evolved its own individual style, which includes a strong element of classical ballet. The company has now

Students of the Royal Ballet School, London, also learn modern dance as part of the much-widened course which also includes many forms of folk dance

founded the Rambert Academy, part of the West London Institute of Higher Education. The Academy offers up to thirty places for a full-time Foundation Course in Dance taking two years. The course includes the usual daily classes in both classical and modern dance as well as a full range of related classes from the study of repertoire to make-up, and drama to stage technique. This course does not lead directly to a degree, but it is planned that a full course will start in 1981 which will end with a Performing Arts or Humanities degree. This is a new approach for Britain as it is theatrical in outlook, but we have yet to see what results are produced. Its first-year students have been impressive, so much so that it is quite likely some will be offered places in dance companies before completing the course. This shows the problem of trying to mix dance training with academic training.

Having some educational qualifications is an obvious advantage for the future, but if you want to be a performer it is not wise to approach your training with one eye on providing something to fall back on if you should fail. This seems to me to increase your chances of failing. Qualifications may have been acquired at the expense of lost opportunities to actually perform. You have to take your chances to dance early otherwise you may find yourself starting out too late. And in dance, especially classical ballet, twenty-one is that much too late.

8 Ken Rinker
Dancer Turned Choreographer

Ken Rinker is an American dancer and choreographer in his mid-thirties, who resides in a 'brownstone' house in Brooklyn, New York. He was born in Washington D.C., and began his career as a dancer quite late while he was at university. He went on to study with both Martha Graham and Merce Cunningham, worked for several years with Twyla Tharp's company and eventually made the decision to turn choreographer. His work includes a musical version of *Alice in Wonderland* for Joe Papp's Public Theatre, with Meryl Streep in the title role (though this only reached rehearsal stage), his first publicly performed musical *Swing* about the big band era and, recently, *Cantata '84: Behind the Moon, Beyond the Rain*.

Ken's first interest in dancing came from watching shows on television as a child, 'Shows like *Ed Sullivan* or *Jackie Gleason and the June Taylor Dancers*. But the real turning point was in high school when I went to see Broadway shows playing at the National Theatre like *My Fair Lady* or *Camelot*. I enjoyed the dancing and thought "boy, that looks like fun and it looks easy, and I like to be physical." And I'd think, "that's what I'd like to try to do." So I saved my lunch money and went to see as many as I could.'

Just before going to college, Ken went to see the New York City Ballet which was performing in Washington in Rock Creek Park. 'They did one week, and they were the first ballet performances I'd seen. I think I went every night. That's when I saw all of the great Balanchine pieces with many of the original creators of the roles dancing them. It was like seeing the Martha Graham or Merce Cunningham compan-

70

ies at their peak. That's when I felt that dance was what I wanted to do.'

At eighteen Ken entered the University of Maryland and there he took his first class in modern dance.

'I didn't know anything about the difference between ballet or modern or jazz, nothing. But to go into a room where there were just floorboards and no furniture, nothing in the middle, and everyone in their black leotards and tights—and *drums*— I suppose you could say it was ritualistic. That turned me on and being physical turned me on. And that was the start.'

After his first year at university Ken was asked by the director of the university dance programme and dance group, Dorothy Madden, to be one of seven students to go to England with her.

'We took dance performances of student choreography around different colleges in order to show the Ministry of Education in England what could be produced in academic institutions, liberal arts colleges and training colleges with the performing arts and, in particular, dance.

'That was a tremendous experience for me because it was the first time I went to Europe, and the first time I did a tour of performing. It caused a great big change in me as a person as well as in my development as a dancer. It was probably one of the real highs of my life because it was a combination of personal pleasure and professional endeavor. It had the right balance between work and play—magically so, because I don't know how it ever happened.'

Although Ken studied English as his main subject at the university, he considered his dancing far more important. 'In my last year I was in a fraternity for good scholarship and leadership and all that, and I thought it was very funny because I didn't take my English as seriously as I did my dance—it was a sideline. Here I was with all these jock types and these intellectual types and I wondered how I got there. I didn't do a lot of studying—I got by, really. I put my hours in on dancing.'

Since they only offered modern dance at Maryland, he decided in his senior year also to attend classes at the National Ballet School in Washington (which no longer exists). 'I decided to do ballet because I was a little bit intimidated by it as a modern dancer, intimidated by the virtuosity of ballet technique. I felt I needed to do it even though it would be hard for me because I was then twenty-two—ancient to start doing ballet. But I was stretched, I had stamina and control in other areas. It was learning the steps that I found very difficult. And then, of course, working on getting the turn-outs as best I could and centering my body. I think the essence of dancing is at its most efficient in ballet. I'm not talking about style. I'm just talking about the basics of a plié, of placing your body properly and all the other things that are indispensable to know in any kind of dancing. That's what I do now to warm up—ballet. And if I do a class I'd rather do a ballet class.'

Although Ken started his dancing late, he feels he was lucky.

'It is hard after your body is formed to try to make it do something that it should have been doing ten years earlier. Some people are given bodies that can assimilate, stretch, turn out. I think I was fortunate enough to have a good body, and I was elastic enough and the muscles were loose enough. Oh, I had things that I should have done better or should have worked on—but I think I was blessed with a physical facility, considering that I started late.'

After graduating from university, Ken earned his living by teaching English at a Junior High School in Baltimore. He continued to study ballet and he also took classes and performed with the company of Ethel Butler, who had danced with Martha Graham in the thirties and forties and who now had a dance group of her own. His schedule was, to put it mildly, busy:

'That year was basically 6:00 a.m. to midnight. I'd get up and allow forty-five minutes to drive to Baltimore to teach (doing about eighty miles an hour), then drive at eighty-five or ninety back down to the National Ballet School to take classes in the afternoon. I'd leave there are about 7:00 p.m., zoom up to Ethel's class, then rehearse with Ethel's company from about 9:00 to midnight.

'But that was an exciting time for me because I was doing the things I wanted to do. Teaching was not one

73

of the things I wanted to do, but it paid my way so I could do these other things. I should have been more scared to death than I was when I started teaching. It wasn't too bad for an "inner city" school—I had one good group, one awful group and two in-between groups. But it was a year when they tested me. One kid threatened to kill me. I did that one year and aged five. It was the only time in my life I dreamed in technicolor.'

In 1969 Ken was invited by the composer Sergio Cervetti to go to Berlin where Cervetti had secured a composer-in-residence post. Ken stayed for a year, doing some teaching in choreography there. He then moved on to New York in 1970. 'When I think about it, it could have been scary because I didn't have a job and I didn't have security. I knew that I wanted to choreograph, but I wanted to dance and to perform more. That's been the root of many good choreographers, to be dancers and performers first. I knew that I wanted to dance; nevertheless I knew that I wanted to be creative and to make my own pieces.'

Thinking back on the time he had so far spent preparing to be a dancer, he weighs the balance between having an academic education first or going immediately for a career in dance.

'I got my foundations at the university, good foundations, and I think I came to New York at the right time because of those foundations. At the same time I was evaluating myself. They didn't offer ballet, but I knew I wanted to take it. There wasn't anybody pushing me to take ballet except myself.

'There is a big difference between professional experience and academic experience. Everything is always a little easier in an academic situation: you can get space a little easier, the teachers aren't as tough on you and you are not as tough on yourself because the competition isn't the same. Professionally the numbers are different. If you come to New York there are a hundred people in a class if you want to work with a good teacher. And the teacher isn't necessarily interested in you. You have to learn to work for yourself. In academic situations they're students, they're still learning. In the professional world you have people who know how to work, know what the goal is—what the focus is.

'There are certain demands that in academic situations just aren't made, but are in the professional world. The fact is that art isn't democratic. A choreographer knows what he wants and should get what he wants. And there's no substitute for the real thing, for working with someone like Balanchine or with a first-class teacher. Individually you have to be very aware of yourself and your needs. I think if I'd come to New York when I was first learning to dance, then I would have been swallowed up, because I wouldn't have had a clear idea of what I wanted to do, with whom I wanted to dance and how I wanted to go about it. In the university I was allowed to develop to the point where I could then make up my mind to study with Martha Graham or Merce Cunningham and so on.

'And I could make up my mind not to say yes to everybody who wanted me to dance with them. Back when I started dancing it was too easy for males— they weren't so numerous. So you have to be smart and decide who to say yes to. If you say yes to everyone, at the end of doing all the performances, what have you learned?'

He feels, however, that his arguments cannot be applied to female dancers so easily. 'In the abstract it really shouldn't matter in terms of what the goal is. But it seems that women get exposed to ballet earlier on, so in some sense they haven't thought about whether they do or don't want to dance. With boys I don't think mothers tend to push their sons into ballet class when they're young; sons have to ask. And I still think there are more good women dancers than good men dancers, so for women it's far more difficult.'

Ken thinks that New York is still the best place for a professional dancer. 'There are small companies in other cities like Atlanta, Boston, and San Francisco. Then there are the modern companies. But it is different. Again, I would say that there is no substitute for the real thing, as good or as bad as it might be. New York has its drawbacks living in crowded conditions—if you don't have a lot of money you can't have a nice place to live—just the quality of life. But I really thought I would be happy living just in a small little room so long as I could go out and

Merce Cunningham, a former partner of Martha Graham, is now the leading creator of the modern dance scene. Over sixty, he still performs and comes up with controversial new ideas which influence much younger dancers and choreographers

dance. Now I don't think I could put up with that.'

Once in New York, he studied for six months at the Martha Graham studio and then got a scholarship and studied for nine months with Merce Cunningham. During this time Ken fell ill, and after a month's recuperation he returned to the Cunningham studio with certain doubts about his career.

'At the time I felt I couldn't find any reason for being there, it just didn't make sense. After some breathing time though, I felt OK and tried to express my sense of having re-discovered what I thought I had lost about the group. But I couldn't communicate this to Merce. Eventually I decided it was the wrong place for me to be. Then I got really down, because I didn't know what I wanted to do. Before I had had a goal—dancing with Merce's company.'

However, Twyla Tharp had seen Ken dancing in Merce's classes. When she heard he had left the studio she asked him to go with her company to Paris, on tour. 'I said, "I'll think about it"' he laughs. 'And then of course I called back the next day and said yes. I wanted to go, but I said I would think about it, not because I didn't want to go to Paris, but why go to Paris just for the sake of going? I wanted to dance and I was lost. So I had to evaluate whether I wanted to work with them. I had never seen any of Twyla's work before. I said yes, and I did it, and I was glad to do it. And I continued to dance with her from '71 until about '76/'77. Those were good times to be working with her and the rest of the dancers in the company. It was a very solid group of people, and stayed about the same practically throughout all that time.'

Ken reflects on what, as a dancer, performance meant to him.

'Sometimes it is a charge. For some performances it's been ecstacy, where you're in another kind of state and you can do more than you thought you could do in rehearsal. Where you can go a little further in balance or turning than you thought you could, or be even more concentrated in the kind of character you've set in your mind.

'You can make sense out of things that are incoherent by making a character for yourself or a story about what you're doing. You may not want to communicate it to the audience, but it will bring something to you that will help the movement make sense and then will put something in the audience's mind about what you're doing, rather than just being a bunch of steps. But there are some pieces where I didn't have justification for what I was doing and therefore I didn't like doing them. They were hard to do.

'Sometimes transitions that didn't happen so well in rehearsal happen better in performance. Then sometimes it can all be turned around, and at the conclusion of a performance that you felt great about someone will say, "Well, it wasn't as good as it was last night." And I had liked what I was doing! Enjoyment is the key. I enjoy it. Not just performance, but rehearsing and taking class.'

During his work with Twyla, Ken thought more and more seriously about becoming a choreographer. By 1974, while he was on tour in London, he had just about made up his mind. 'I had a big internal discussion with myself as to when it would be. I knew then that I had fulfilled what I wanted to do in terms of dancing and performing. I wanted to go on to make my own dances. But I'm kind of slow, not in making my mind up, but in seizing the right moment. It took two years to find the right time to get out of the dancing.'

Ken joined Twyla as her assistant choreographer for the film *Hair*. When he worked on the two musicals, *Alice* and *Swing*, he found the task exciting and, certainly, educational. 'I benefited from having the experience without the exposure, in both situations, because if you aren't publicly put on display or criticized yet, it means you can still experiment. You can feel as though it's more or less time in a lab rather than being up front so that, in a way, you can still concern yourself with the process, the development of the piece. For me, as a beginner in the theatre, even though the experience took its toll in other ways, it was beneficial in that respect.

'I was given opportunities to choreograph based on who I was as a dancer. Last year I did a piece based musically and thematically on the song and movie *42nd Street*, called *40 Second/42nd Variations*. Meaning there was a forty second theme that I presented with forty-two variations. Now everybody calls it

42nd Street, which is what I intended but didn't say in the title. That's one of the things that interests me as an artist, to plant things like Hitchcock would but not demonstrate it. People will see it. My piece was about making the piece. I played the guy who was the choreographer. One of the things I wanted to say was "Here I am as a choreographer, not as a dancer anymore." And it was successful beyond my wildest dreams. Out of just that I was asked to do a Broadway show. I was surprised, shocked . . . amazed!'

Ken thinks that, nowadays, choreographic styles are much harder to fit into certain moulds. 'There's

Ken Rinker
demonstrates his limber
facility in this energetic
dance movement

such a mix of styles and approaches that it's hard to say it's purely this or that. There don't seem to be any big breaks with tradition like there were in the thirties, like Isadora Duncan, because we've already done that. My personal feeling is that we've gone down too many different alleys already, and I'm all for amalgamating, saying it's OK to take this and to take that and make something new by juxtaposition. Now I think it's time to recognize the similarities and dissimilarities of all these traditions and bring them together. That's why I want to choreograph, because I feel that I have something to say.'

Financially, life isn't that easy. 'To tell you the truth, I am not really earning an income that will "keep me in the style" I'd like. If I were still dancing, working with Twyla, then I would be. The money I make is out of choreography and teaching and that isn't very much.'

He also wishes that he, and the performing arts in general, were not so dependent on grants.

'That's the way it is, and I don't like it. I've been freelance, Twyla's assistant on *Hair* and doing Joe Papp's Public Theater. Now I'm in a transition period. Do I want to go on doing that or make my own group? I don't really want to make my own group because I don't believe that's the wave of the future. Everyone going down their own alley again. So I'm balking. But I have to survive choreographically. And if I incorporate I can get government support—more funding. I don't know if I want to incorporate. Ideally, I'd like to do a Broadway show that would run for a few years and sustain me. But commercial things don't always allow you to go out on a limb and be experimental, and I'm in that position now, where I want to experiment.

Although Ken misses the dancing, he feels he doesn't have the time or physical stamina to return to class, and he has no desire to return to dance professionally.

'No, I feel as though I've done that. It's like getting a red wagon at Christmas when you're seven. I've had that, and now I want something else.

'When I go to performances I'm not just looking at the dancers. I'm looking at *dance*—the piece up there—the content.'

9 Theatre School

Many dancers receive their training in a theatre school, rather than one specializing in ballet. These schools provide all-round theatrical training including acting, singing and all forms of dance. With very few exceptions these schools are privately run and not attached to particular companies. They are the equivalent of the big private ballet schools.

The major schools in Britain and America in particular have a very high standard and many major stars of the musical stage received their training there. Perhaps the most famous school is the School of the Performing Arts in New York. Its work was put on film in *Fame*, though this was a little fanciful in its outlook. It did however show the range of activities, from modern dance to mathematics, as well as the hectic life a student has. This school only

An audition for the High School of Performing Arts, New York, as shown in the film *Fame*

takes older pupils, in the seventeen and upwards age range, whereas most schools, particularly those in Britain, take students much younger with pupils joining often as early as seven or eight.

Most schools take children in through auditions and reports of general academic ability, though that is not as important as in ordinary schools. In Britain they are inspected regularly by the Ministry of Education to make sure that the teaching is of the required standard.

Life at these schools is a mixture of the magic of the theatre and the hard work of the classroom. As with the university courses I have already mentioned, life is particularly hard as there is such a strong physical element. After the daily dance class which can last an hour and a half (though it is often shorter when the pupil is not specializing in ballet) pupils will have an ordinary day's academic schooling alongside other classes in theatre work; singing, mime, acting, tap and jazz dance. Some may then go on to a theatre where they will be appearing in a commercial show.

Young Performers

Many of the children in these schools are in demand as models, as well as sometimes appearing in musicals, plays, films or television commercials. The children you see advertising a product are young 'professionals' and not just someone found in the street by the producer! These activities are controlled by the various city authorities to make sure that the children are not overworked or exploited. This means that a particularly talented child such as Anne Marie Gwatkin, who took the leading role in *Annie* in the London production, can have a great success with wonderful newspaper reviews and a lot of applause, but she is only allowed to do a certain number of performances no matter how successful she is. Once her yearly quota is full she has to return to her school and wait before appearing in another show.

Some children are so successful in getting parts in shows, plays or commercials that they can easily pay their own school fees or put quite a lot away for the future, which in the theatre can be very uncertain especially when a young dancer or actor is trying to

Lena Zavaroni, a young pupil of the Italia Conti Stage School, who, by the time she was 13, had had major television shows and was rapidly becoming as accomplished at dancing and appearing on talk shows as she had always been as a singer

establish a career. There are of course even young 'stars' to be found in these schools, children of twelve and thirteen who already have made major television appearances and played many leading parts. Two of the biggest young musical stars in Britain were in the same class at the Italia Conti Stage School: Lena Zavaroni and Bonnie Langford. Lena won an important talent show on television at the age of nine with her strong voice and after training developed into an excellent all-round entertainer with a television series of her own. Bonnie made her name on the stage and was a great success when she starred with Angela Lansbury in *Gypsy* in London. Her tap dancing stopped the show every night. She then toured with the show across America and had a similar success there. Both these young performers have now left the classroom and at sixteen and fifteen respectively are full professionals. They have even made an hour long television show together, suitably called *Lena and Bonnie* and are wonderfully competent and very funny performers on television talk shows.

This confidence is something which children at

theatre schools seem to have plenty of! Working alongside equally talented and ambitious children they have to have it and it is good training for the difficult profession they are going to enter. They also have to get used to the not very pleasant business of attending auditions at a very early age and have to accept the fact that they may well not be chosen for even a tiny part in the chorus. This is often the time when confidence breaks and there may be the occasional outburst of tears, but they are soon forgotten.

An audition can often be specially difficult for children. They will perform their party piece and do their favourite dance, but the danger is to do it mechanically, to be over-rehearsed. Directors who are taking the audition have the difficult job of looking for someone they can work with on a role and not someone with a very set way of singing and dancing. They are also looking for children with the stamina to cope with their school work as well as several weeks rehearsal before the show, always the most difficult and testing time.

Even while the show is going on children are not excused their academic work and are carefully looked after in the theatre. Teachers come from their school or the theatre company will employ one specially for them to give lessons in between the matinee and evening performances for example or to supervise some revision or homework if the children are not needed for a whole act during the perform-ance.

Children from theatre schools have usually had much more performing experience by the time they go out into the world to look for work than pupils from a ballet school. *Their* performing may have been limited to their own school shows or performing for some local charity event which is not the same as regular appearances on Broadway or in London's West End. Children from the major ballet schools attached to companies will have had some experience on stage as extras with that company or some of the most senior girls may have been given the oppor-tunity to go on stage as one of the last ballerinas in *La Bayadère*, always a nerve-racking experience.

Once children leave a theatre school their life is not

Students from the Royal Ballet School have their own performances in several small theatres around London, as well as their own big matinee performance at the Royal Opera House

as ordered as it will be for ballet students. Apart from whatever academic qualifications they may have there are no special diplomas which will guarantee them work. Prospective employers have to see what they can do in auditions or in performances their agent will find for them, probably away from a main centre. Even finding an agent may not be particularly easy, and it is vital to have one you can trust and who will promote your career and look for good opportunities for you. While a ballet dancer is secure once inside a company, the theatre dancer will have to settle for what work may come his way; one week a television show, six weeks of pantomime at Christmas, six weeks without any work at all. And then a producer or choreographer remembers seeing you in some small part and thinks how perfect you would be for a new big musical. The first step in a career as a solo performer. Even a star!

Popular Dance Forms

10

Disco

The world of professional disco dancing is new, glamorous and looks great fun from the outside. In reality it is a tiny, highly competitive and often unrewarding world. There are groups specializing in disco styles and even whole travelling shows made up of the winners of various disco competitions, but it is not a career that it is sensible to train for. As an additional source of work and income it might be useful for a short time, but except for a World Disco Champion it promises a brief career of only a few years.

Most of the dance groups who perform disco routines draw their members from regular ballet and theatre schools, and these dancers are often very versatile and ready to dance other styles in other shows. Disco dancers, on the other hand, tend to have their one speciality and as soon as it becomes unfashionable they will find themselves out of work.

When you see a group doing a disco routine you can be sure that their spontaneous look has been as carefully and painstakingly rehearsed as a variation in classical ballet. To do this type of dance professionally it has to be remembered and performed equally well many times over, and it also requires the ability to dance with a partner. All the basic techniques of disco dancing can be learned better at a ballet or even a jazz class.

There are, of course, many talented amateurs in the big disco competitions which are shown on television. By the time the various regional competitions have finished, however, a high proportion of the dancers are only 'amateur' in the sense

that they are not making a full-time living from
dancing, usually they have all had some sort of dance
training. Those who are truly amateur often have a
great talent, but it is all too often a talent to do only
one thing. If they find they can do the splits easily,
their disco routine will involve doing just that, very
often. Others may have an ability to turn, but any
dance student will see that they are really spinning
and not doing controlled turns. They do not 'spot' to
avoid getting dizzy and would probably be quite
incapable of doing a long routine or of coping with a
partner.

Over the years fun dances as well as folk dances
have been turned into theatrical dances. The Polka
and the Charleston swept Europe and America. Rock
and roll started in the dance hall, but was soon taken
up by films and television. These dances seldom last
long. They are popular crazes but, especially today,
are soon out of date. In a few years time will you
remember the Bump or the Robot?

Ballroom Dancing
Some people have always made a living out of
ballroom dancing, either teaching or demonstrating

it, but more probably from organizing it. It is a dance form which can still provide a reasonable, even a very good income, especially for national champions who turn professional.

The most famous professional dancers of this century were the American couple Vernon and Irene Castle who popularized dances in the early 1900s. They did demonstrations in smart hotels and at private parties, inventing new dances which would, be the rage for a while. Their life story was turned into a film for Fred Astaire and Ginger Rogers.

No one, however, is likely to set out to make ballroom dancing a career. It is much more probable that first of all you will do it for fun at a local dance school. You may then find you have an aptitude for it and if you are lucky, will find a partner with whom you work particularly well. This a dance form which thrives on competition, and as soon as you are proficient the organizer of your dance school should enter you for local and then national competitions. It is difficult to advise how to find the right dance school, as it depends on where you live, but you will find advertisements in the various ballroom dancing magazines and if there is a good school in your area they are quite likely to recommend it.

If you find that you like competing, whether as a couple or as part of a formation dance team, you might decide to aim for the top, but at the same time you will be doing your normal work. Training for this type of dance can never be a full-time occupation.

Training for competitions will be as arduous as any ballet rehearsal and it is not surprising to find that many ballet steps have found their way into the more complicated dances. When you become polished you will also realize how little professional ballroom dancing has to do with dancing for pleasure. The dances which originated in the ballroom the Foxtrot, the Tango or even the Waltz, have become stylized in exactly the same way as folk dance and ballet.

The world of the professional ballroom dancer now includes new social dances and if a particular disco dance is very popular special versions of it will be developed for exhibitions. Professional ballroom dancing involves endless travel from one town to another giving demonstration dances, though there

can be longer periods of teaching. It can be a very
short career, however, unless you eventually set up
your own successful school, for new champions will
win the major competitions.

Once dancers from Great Britain were totally
supreme but now they are being challenged by
dancers from Japan and Australia in particular.
There is even growing interest in ballroom dancing
in America which will no doubt give greater scope for
the professional dancer in the future.

Ice Dance

Ice dancers are usually skaters first and dancers
second. It is extremely rare for trained ballet dancers
to make the switch, for the simple reason that while
learning ballet it is rather dangerous to indulge in
sports like skating or skiing. Broken limbs and
dancing do not go together.

Nowadays, ice shows such as *Holiday on Ice* or *Ice
Capades* employ literally hundreds of skaters who
have to take part in routines ranging from excerpts
from Broadway musicals to balletic sequences, or are
just used to make up colourful spectacles. The most
recent trend is for a much wider range of dance than
before, when the emphasis was on magnificent
costume and massed effect.

In the 1930s and 1940s there were spectacular ice
skating films starring Sonje Henie, but these have
long since gone out of fashion since the stories which
were invented as an excuse for the skating were very
weak, rather like those that were thought up as an
excuse for Esther Williams to swim. These films did,
however, bring skating to a wide public. Before that
time there had been ice shows ranging from a musical
comedy called the *Arabian Nights* in Britain in 1932 to
one at the Royal Opera House, Covent Garden!

Ballet on Skates

The introduction of dance and ballet steps into ice
skating has recently captured the public imagination. Usually the stars of these shows start as
winners of major international championships, the
World title or the Olympic title for instance, though
now a few start in the chorus and work their way up.

The influence of classical ballet on ice skating was

first shown in an effective way by the Protopovs from Russia, who skated in Pair Skating events. They were World Champions as well as winners of the Olympic Gold medal on two occasions. The routines which were worked out for them were heavily influenced by the bravura Russian ballet style with wonderful lifts and good line. They also used more interesting music than had been heard before, often excerpts from ballets, though this did not please ballet enthusiasts as they were usually badly edited and did not sound their best over loudspeakers.

From these beginnings ballet began to influence ice dancing events which previously had been based firmly on ballroom steps and strictly supervised by the controlling authority. Even so, the couples are only allowed to introduce more personal elements in the free dance section and then they are very restricted as to how many turns they can do, how high the girl can be lifted or how far apart they are allowed to skate.

The great breakthrough came in the Men's Individual skating events when John Curry based his routines firmly on ballet. Given the limitations of

John Curry, European, World and Olympic figure skating champion, brought the balletic idea of line into skating. By the time he won the championships he had also introduced actual ballet steps, simple beats and jumps as well as extensive use of balletic ports de bras

89

heavy skating boots, the fact that in skating the feet are parallel and not turned out, as well as the fact that for most jumps the skater takes off backwards, Curry managed to introduce actual ballet steps as well as a ballet style very successfully. Appropriately his most famous and most balletic routine, with which he won the World and Olympic championships, was based on the *Don Quixote* pas de deux.

Since that time almost every skater has introduced a much greater sense of style into 'performances' at championship events. It is significant that good ports de bras in the free section can now mean the difference between a gold or silver medal.

John Curry, like most medal-winners, turned professional and started his own ice show which is based in a theatre rather than an ice rink. He invited great ballet choreographers ranging from Kenneth MacMillan to Twyla Tharp to create ballets for his small group. Sadly it has not met with the enormous success of the more spectacular shows as audiences still expect triple jumps and multiple spins as well as the artistic displays. This suits a champion like Robin Cousins perfectly. Heavily influenced by Curry though in no way copying him, Cousins has found a natural style which can easily combine the spectacular steps, and he jumps quite remarkably high, with disco dance styles.

Cousins now dances with an ice show and expects to do up to twelve performances a week, even more at holiday times. For this a dancer of his ability, perhaps someone like Dorothy Hamill in America or Toller Cranston in Canada, can expect to earn upwards of $120,000 (£50,000) a year, not to mention the extra money to be made from advertising sports products or making television shows.

These fantastic figures are of course not available to the hard-working corps de ballet (corps de glace?) who skate behind the stars. Nonetheless a good living can be made. The shows are constantly auditioning for new skaters, and the technical requirements are not particularly demanding as the most spectacular steps will be danced by the stars. Most of the shows have more than one company touring and it can be a marvellous way of seeing the world while doing what you enjoy most.

Patti Hammond
Classical to Cabaret

11

'In my sort of job you have to be able to do everything. You have to change easily from one dance style to another. You have to learn routines very quickly. You have to change the way you perform to suit the impersonal atmosphere of a television studio or a cabaret audience sitting almost under your nose. In every way I am very grateful for the discipline of my classical ballet training.'

Patti Hammond is a member of one of the most popular dance groups in Britain, Legs and Co. They appear every week on the top-rating record show *Top of the Pops* as well as in cabaret, where they perform their forty-five minute, all-dance programme.

Patti has been a member of other popular dance groups including the Second Generation and Ruby Flipper, but started her career as a dancer with the Royal Ballet, followed by a period with London Festival Ballet. Her career has covered the whole world of dance.

I was particularly interested to find out why she made the change from the world of classical ballet to that of popular dance on television and in the theatre as I knew that she had done well with the London Festival Ballet and had been given many opportunities and several good roles. She told me 'Yes, I was doing very well. The Director liked me and visiting choreographers used me. I had no special reason to suddenly change direction, but over a period I became unhappy with classical ballet. But I should say that it was more a case of becoming unhappy with the life of a classical dancer than with the actual dancing. My decision was to leave ballet life, rather than to take up another form of dancing. I felt that ballet was taking

A publicity shot for the dance group Legs & Co with Patti Hammond (second from right)

me over completely and I felt that I was losing my identity.'

This feeling will be very recognizable to anyone who is studying ballet or has just joined a company. Classical ballet requires total dedication and really is more a way of life than a job. It leaves little time for socializing outside of the company and students miss out on many of the opportunities other children have as the ballet studies are not only physically demanding, but also are extra to normal schoolwork.

Patti was born in Hong Kong, but came to Britain as a very young child. Her mother was born in China and had a theatrical background, indeed after coming to Britain she appeared in such famous musicals as *The World of Suzie Wong* and *The Flower Drum Song*. But there was no family pressure for Patti to start dancing. 'In the first town we lived I went along with other kids to a ballet class. I wasn't particularly interested. In fact, looking back I think I actually disliked it. I know I never went back. Then we moved to a different area and I went along to the local ballet school which also taught acrobatics. Loved the acrobatics, but still didn't take much interest in the ballet. Now I think about it, I was there because a doctor had told my parents that dance lessons would help straighten out my bow legs!

Anyway, my ballet teacher thought that I had a natural talent, so good that she suggested that I try to get into the Royal Ballet School when I was only eight. I don't think I really knew fully what this meant at the time. I certainly didn't have any idea of what it might lead to. I never thought of dancing as a career until I got into the school. I was spoilt there a little as I was the baby of the school having been accepted under the age limit of that time. Once in the school I got hooked on ballet.'

This early in Patti's career there was an element of luck and also showed her natural ability to adapt, even if it was done very innocently. 'I thought I'd audition for White Lodge [the Royal Ballet Junior School] as there didn't seem much chance of getting in as I was under age. On top of this I was better at dancing instinctively than at the technical side, though naturally I had completed the usual grade exams. So along we went, late as I remember it. We had trouble with the car and I got very upset in case we should miss it, which is a bit odd as I don't remember caring that much! Well, we got there in time, I did the audition. At the barre the teachers were interested in me as I did very high arabesques, much higher than the English style. Fortunately I am naturally loose and I had been doing the acrobatics classes. I also remember being asked to do some free dance in the centre, but when the music played nothing came into my head so I just did my own version of what the girl in front of me was doing. It was good enough and I was offered a place.'

Patti as a student at the Royal Ballet School

There were some small problems to overcome as Patti's parents had not really planned for this, but fortunately with the help of a grant and the whole family rallying round she was able to join the school.

The training at the Royal Ballet School concentrated entirely on classical ballet, with only a few classes in folk dance and Spanish dance. Now the course, in the Upper School particularly, is much wider, reflecting the change in dance styles and the demands made on dancers. After graduating into the Upper School, Patti played the usual small parts in ballets at the Opera House, which are invaluable for gaining stage experience, and was very fortunate to have a major part created for her in a new ballet for the School performance there.

The aim of every dancer at the Royal Ballet School is to get a place in the Royal Ballet Company. As it happened the year Patti graduated there were very few places available. She was warned well in advance and remembers feeling totally shattered when told that there was no chance of getting in the company. 'But one day I was sitting outside the ballet studio feeling very miserable indeed when I saw John Field who directed the Touring Company of the Royal Ballet [now the Sadler's Wells Royal Ballet]. On impulse I stopped him and asked him if there was a place in his company for me. He seemed a little surprised that I should ask as he had already asked for me, but word hadn't reached me. You can imagine how I felt. One moment completely unhappy, the next overjoyed.'

Perhaps even in these early days she was starting to have the thoughts which would eventually make her leave the world of classical ballet. 'It seems that dancers are always a bit like children, depending so much on praise and encouragement from everyone. You get upset if a rehearsal doesn't go well. Then you are happy because you see that you have been cast to dance some nice role. Next moment you are shattered because the Director makes some unfavourable comment about your performance. I remember so well when I was in Festival Ballet. The director, Beryl Grey, liked me and encouraged me, but when she made some small criticism I'd be so unhappy, out of all proportion to what she said.'

Patti was in the Royal Ballet for only one year when there was a change of policy regarding the Touring Company and she and other dancers found themselves out of work. At this time she got her first experience of the commercial theatre as one of the Royal Ballet's young choreographers, Geoffrey Cauley, was asked to do a musical. He naturally wanted to work with dancers he knew which meant that Patti got a part. She also got her first taste of the uncertainty of commercial work. The musical closed after a couple of performances and Patti had to find other work. At this time she still wanted to dance classical ballet and was very fortunate to be allowed to go back to the Royal Ballet School to take classes there. She was then advised that it might be a good thing for her future if she was to try to get into London Festival Ballet. As it happened the reasons for this advice turned out to be wrong, but things did not work out too badly. As Patti says, 'It sounds like a typical theatrical sob story, but this is quite true. I had spent almost all the money I had going to Southampton where Festival Ballet were appearing. I asked if I could do class with the company and was given permission. After a few days when I thought that the ballet masters and director had had a chance to see my work I asked Beryl Grey if there was a chance of joining the company. She seemed to like my work and said she was sure she would find me a place sooner or later, but did not know when a vacancy would come about. It was nice to be liked, but I was still unhappy as I really couldn't afford to wait. I went to the dressing-room to have a little cry! One of the dancers, to whom I really should be very grateful, told me that if it meant so much to me I should go straight back to Miss Grey and explain my position exactly. So I did. I told her that I had to have something more definite than a general promise as I had no money and would have to take a job somewhere. To my surprise she sat right down with her ballet master and went through the company list to see who might stay and who might go, as I stood there. And then she offered me a contract!'

Once in the company she found good opportunities, but still had those nagging thoughts about being totally dedicated to classical ballet to the exclusion of everything else. She thought that a lot of a dancers seemed genuinely unhappy and had no time for relationships outside the company. But as she was given roles she worked hard. As she said earlier she still liked the dancing, it was the life which bothered her. At the same time she realized that as she was an interpretive dancer rather than a technical one she would probably reach her peak in the company fairly soon and life might become an endless succession of Swans and Wilis. Being a member of a corps de ballet really can mean a loss of identity, for everyone must be more or less the same.

When Denis Nahat, the American choreographer, came to Festival Ballet to mount his *Mendelssohn*

Patti dances with John
Travis in a London
Festival Ballet
performance,
Mendelssohn Symphony

Symphony he chose her for a solo part and a difficult,
technical solo part at that. She worked well with him
and he worked her very hard. She did technical

96

things she never thought she would achieve, but at the same time knew that she had reached her technical limits. She is quite sure that she made a pretty realistic decision about this and did not just 'throw in the towel'. The hard work with Nahat had pushed her to physical as well as technical limits. As she had a continuous health problem she soon took a leave of absence to have her tonsils out. She decided during this period to make the break with classical ballet.

Then there was the problem of earning a living. She still wanted to dance so that more or less left only one thing to do, take up theatrical dance. There are so many different possibilities in the field of theatre and television that it is essential to work with a good agent, even several agents, if you plan to model or do television commercials. It also helps if you can work with one of the top choreographers. Patti set about approaching agents and was lucky enough to be taken on by a top model agency, as well as by a management company run by a choreographer, Douglas Squires. He had been very important in raising the general level of dancing on television and had formed a very influential dance group, The Younger Generation. He was very interested in ballet and used many balletic ideas in his choreography. It seems natural that he should like Patti, though in the overcrowded world of theatre dance liking is often not enough. You have to be a superb dancer as well. Patti set about learning the different techniques of theatre dancing, though as she says, it was just as much a case of unlearning some of the classical postures, freeing the body, carrying herself in a different, apparently more relaxed way. She worked with the best teachers of jazz dancing as well as Squires himself and soon was appearing in his television shows as well as landing other parts on the stage, including the part of Tiger Lily in the famous production of *Peter Pan*. She also featured in one of the first all dance feature films, but for various commercial reasons it is unfortunately still unshown. Had it been 'I'd have been a star by now,' she says with tongue firmly in cheek!

The role of Tiger Lily might have had something to do with her slightly oriental features, features which

97

have wasted a bit of her time. She was often approached to audition for oriental roles, geisha girls and the like, only to arrive and be told that she wasn't oriental enough. Fortunately for her she did not have many experiences like that; one of the benefits of having worked with good agents and choreographers. If a management approaches a good agent whom they trust, the dancer starts with an advantage at an audition. Sometimes the audition is only a formality. This can save many hours of fruitless travel or waiting around in dance studios.

During this period Patti was busy working with various groups, modelling and trying to make other opportunities for herself. She is a firm believer in going out to look for opportunities and has never expected them to turn up by themselves. She seems to be so busy when she rattles off the things she has done that her life seems at least as full and committed as the ballet life she was trying to get away from. She sees it quite differently, 'The things I am talking about are largely practical, writing off for auditions, posing for sample photographs for agents, attending auditions. At least you are out and about meeting a much wider range of people. You are also not dancing every night unless you get a part in a successful West End or Broadway show. You have more nights off. And then the dancing isn't really so demanding.' I immediately took this point up. If it is less demanding is it less rewarding and creative than ballet? 'Definitely not. I know we are not creating great characters or great dramas but we have to work just as hard to present ourselves on stage and to do what the choreographer gives us to the best of our ability. If you are honest and try to do your best I don't see any difference between a back row Swan or one of six girls dancing for an audience of millions. It suits me very well as I like being me up there, dancing, and not an anonymous dancer heavily made-up hiding behind some character part. We also do an incredibly varied amount of work. Pop music today covers such an enormous range and to add to the excitement of our particular job, Legs and Co have no idea what they will be dancing from week to week. It has to be a record going up the charts, but that can mean a piece of heavy rock, a ballad or a classical piece that has become popular through being a film or television theme. We recently did a very classically based dance to the theme from *The Deer Hunter*. Next moment we could be all punk! To make our life, and the life of our choreographer Flick Colby, just a bit more difficult, if the piece we are working on should slip in the charts the day before we record, we prepare a whole new number.'

This all seems to be too good to be true. Is there anything she does miss? 'Yes. Having come up through the ballet, then working with Dougie Squires and The Second Generation [the second group he formed] and then Ruby Flipper I have been used to working with boys. Now the fashion is for all girl groups and I feel a whole part of dance is missing. I enjoy double work, lifts, all that sort of thing. The other snag is the general lack of work. I've been very lucky. While working for Dougie, someone in the wardrobe department of BBC Television suggested I write to Ruby Flipper and I did and was successful. From this has grown the work I am doing now. But if I was not so identified with a particular group and had to work from one small job to another I really would have to keep on the move. There just aren't the opportunities in Britain that exist in America.'

Are there any major differences or problems in dancing for television? 'Of course there are differences,' says Patti, 'especially if you have been used to a live audience. I miss an audience reaction still, but of course we do cabaret, an exhausting forty-five minute cabaret act, in which there is plenty of audience contact. But then you have got those forty-five minutes to get the audience on your side. On television we have two and a half minutes, quite cold, to make our effect. The piece has to be very tightly choreographed and Flick is in a way directing the dance for television as well as choreographing the steps. She has to know her camera angles and all that sort of thing. We work on a very, very tight schedule. Roughly it gives one day for Flick to choose a piece from those suggested by the producer, discuss her idea with the designer and start work on her own dance ideas. She comes to our first rehearsal with the whole thing pretty well worked out. This suits me fine as I feel I'm not a particularly creative person. I just think of myself as a body, a tool for the choreographer to work with. Making new ballets, for instance, the choreographer often asks the dancer to put in ideas or try things out. I suppose we haven't got the time for this approach anyway. After two days rehearsal we are ready for a camera rehearsal and then we shoot it. Unless, of course, as I said before, the record slips in the charts and we have to start all over again. Dancing to the camera isn't a great problem, but you have to judge your performance carefully and not overdo the smiling! Its very easy to oversell yourself.'

As with all forms of popular dancing the essence is to make it look relaxed and easy. This naturally leads far too many people into thinking that it really is relaxed and easy, whereas in real life the routines are as carefully rehearsed and planned as a classical pas de deux. 'We do get a fair bit of mail,' Patti says, 'from people who want to join us because it looks so easy that they think they can do it themselves. We also get mail from people who criticize us for doing such 'simple' things. If only they knew! It looks easy but you'd be amazed how technical it is, and I don't particularly mean the steps. It's the music. When dancing classical ballet dancers count beats, but they are fairly conventional beats which can almost become part of you, so that in a way you do dance along with the music. With so much pop music today the beats are incredibly complicated. I am counting all the time. I don't know how I manage to smile at the same time. At least now we don't have to sing along as well, though oddly enough I didn't find learning that technique too difficult. For some reason people also think the steps are easy, too, but I can tell you the combinations which Flick devises are often as difficult as any in classical ballet. I'm sure we're not having too high an opinion of ourselves, but when we get letters from young people who are great disco dancers and want to join the group we can only tell them that it's not as easy as it looks and that they will need training as well as a natural talent to do the latest fashionable disco dances for a living.'

It is always unfair to ask a dancer what they expect to do next, but equally hard to resist. Patti is quite frank in admitting that you can't go on doing her type of dancing indefinitely any more than you can in the world of ballet. If you are in close-up on a television screen you are treated more harshly than if you are in a theatre wearing a carefully arranged and fairly heavy make-up, yards and yards away from the nearest member of the audience. From the point of dance technique of course she could go on dancing for quite a time, 'If you have the physique and your body stays flexible there shouldn't be a problem,' says Patti, 'and I have the advantage of being naturally very loose, remember my acrobatics! Like a classical dancer we have to keep in condition. Unlike a classical dancer training is largely left to us as we are responsible professional people. I did lessons with many teachers and Dougie Squires gave a class including a barre for his group. We always do a warm-up before working, it's only sensible to avoid accidents. My main worry is not with the dancing, though, it is the fact that I am not a creator. Most dancers who stay in dance go on to do something creative, teaching or choreographing. In that way I haven't changed since my Royal Ballet School audition. I've had wonderful teachers from Dame Ninette de Valois to Pamela May to Maryon Lane. Even after all this time what they taught is still up here in my head. The problem is, getting it out! I don't see myself choreographing. I could branch out into acting, but in many ways that means starting again, learning different techniques, making new contacts. I really can't tell you anything definite.'

This uncertainty is special to the world of dance whether in ballet or television studio, as there is not another profession which faces its members with this decision at a fairly early age. It seems that if you plan a career in dance you have to have nerves of steel because you are going to be faced more than once with a time of decision. You have to be able to go through periods of regular unemployment without losing heart. And then you have to know how to take the next opportunity when it comes. This takes great self-confidence. Judging on the evidence of the three major changes in Patti's career so far and the way she coped with them and turned them all into successes, the lack of a definite answer to the question 'What next?' seems much less important than at first sight.

Dame Ninette de Valois, who built up the great British national company, The Royal Ballet, has also been an influential teacher of many young dancers such as Patti Hammond. Madame, as she is always known, is shown here as a Peasant Woman in her own ballet *Barabau* in 1936

12 Who's Who in Dance

This is a short and selective list of people who have in their different ways opened up the performing world for the dancer this century. There are choreographers; dancers who made a special contribution apart from the brilliance of their dancing; writers who have influenced dance, and several figures who have brought dance to a wider audience. You will not find many of the great dancers of today in this list as you can see them in theatres and find out about their lives from programmes or dictionaries.

Frederick Ashton was born in Ecuador in 1904 and saw Anna Pavlova dance in Lima, Peru when he was thirteen. He decided then that he wanted to dance and went to London to take lessons with Marie Rambert and others. He is important to the dancer as he founded the English style of dancing and gave brilliant opportunities to dancers in his ballets such as *Symphonic Variations* and the ever-popular *La Fille Mal Gardée*. His early ballets such as *A Wedding Bouquet*, *Façade* and *Les Patineurs* are still performed frequently. In 1980, at the age of seventy-six, he created his latest work, *Rhapsody*, in honour of the eightieth birthday of the Queen Mother.

Fred Astaire was born in 1899 and had little dance training as he and his sister, Adele, started out as a variety act when he was seven. By the time he was twenty he had appeared in musical comedy and become an established star in London and New York. He made his first film in 1933 with Joan Crawford, but he is best known for the series of films he made throughout the 1930s with Ginger Rogers. His perfectly controlled and elegant style, coupled with

Ginger Rogers and Fred Astaire in the film *Carefree*

brilliant tap dancing, was shown to perfection in *Top Hat*. His dance routines are as formal as classical pas de deux and he rehearsed them extensively by himself, working out every last detail, before he started work with his partner. This sense of perfection is obvious in all his routines. His films are often shown on television and he still makes occasional appearances and can demonstrate his unique relaxed style.

Josephine Baker was born in America in 1906 and died in Paris in 1975. She was a chorus member of revues at famous Harlem nightclubs in the 1920s before going to Paris with the Black Revue in 1925. At that time composers and choreographers of the classical ballet were heavily influenced by jazz and jazz dancing. Though her work was mostly in the Folies Bergère and the Casino she also worked with George Balanchine who choreographed musicals and other shows in the 1930s. She was one of the first performers to show that 'black is beautiful', and at times she took great delight in doing outrageous dances in fantastic costumes.

George Balanchine was born in St Petersburg (Leningrad) in 1904 and today, at the age of seventy-seven, directs the New York City Ballet, which was largely his creation. He is important because he founded the American style of dance out of the classical school of St Petersburg in which he was brought up. In 1924 he became ballet master with Diaghilev and created several fashionable works before he choreographed two modern classics. *Prodigal Son* and *Apollo*. From the early years of American ballet we also have *Serenade*, which he

Josephine Baker in what the publicity described as a whirlwind of silk, feathers, songs and dances. This is one of her more modest dresses!

103

created for his first students. The school he founded with Lincoln Kirstein is now the School of American Ballet.

Cyril Beaumont was born in London in 1891 and died in 1976. He was a close friend of many famous dance personalities who visited his little bookshop for over fifty years. He was one of the first influential writers on ballet in this century and worked with the great teacher Enrico Cecchetti to write down his famous teaching syllabus.

Busby Berkeley was rather more important to the art of dance than to the individual dancer. In fact it cannot have been a particularly rewarding experience to take part in one of his fantastic creations in films such as *42nd Street*, *Footlight Parade* or the *Gold Diggers* series. Born in 1895 he was a dancer in Broadway shows before he went to Holywood in 1930. He created dances which could only be done on film: the famous kaleidoscope effects seen from above and the simple repeating patterns which used props such as candelabras, ostrich fans and even, on one occasion, moving pianos. He died in 1976 having lived long enough to see his work become fashionable with a new generation.

Erik Bruhn was born in Copenhagen in 1928 and like most Danish dancers studied at the famous school in the Royal Theatre. He was the most stylish classical dancer of his day, mostly in the 1950s and early '60s, as well as excelling in the Bournonville style. He was a wonderful model for many young male dancers, in particular Rudolf Nureyev who much admired him. He now produces ballets for companies such as American Ballet Theater and makes occasional appearances in character roles such as Dr Coppélius or Madge the Witch in *La Sylphide*.

Leslie Caron started out as a ballerina in France and was one of a group of ballerinas who caught the public imagination in musical films such as *An American in Paris* with Gene Kelly and *Daddy Long Legs* with Fred Astaire. She then made a successful change to being an actress.

Jean Cocteau the great French poet and artist was born in 1889. There is a famous story that when he first met the young Cocteau, Diaghilev merely said 'Astonish me!' Cocteau took up the challenge and produced many unusual and controversial ideas for ballets. His later films such as *Orpheus* used mime and looked choreographed rather than directed.

John Cranko was one of the young choreographers to emerge from the Sadler's Wells Ballet, the immediate predecessor of the Royal Ballet. His witty early works took ballet into the commercial theatre in revues and his later full-length works gave wonderful character roles to dancers. He also established the major German ballet company in Stuttgart before his death in 1973 at the age of fifty-six. *Romeo and Juliet*, *Onegin* and *The Taming of the Shrew* are in the repertoires of many companies.

Merce Cunningham is still the most influential performer and creator on the modern dance scene, though now over sixty. He was originally a dancer with Martha Graham, but soon broke away to start his experiments with the relation of movement to music which have continued up to the present day.

Agnes de Mille who was born in New York in 1909, danced in London after her training, but since then she has become a particularly American choreographer. Though she has created many famous works for ballet companies, some using American themes for the first time, her real importance was her transformation of the musical. Her dream ballet in *Oklahoma* in 1943 was a breakthrough, the first time dance had been used to advance the story of a musical and not just for diversion. She went on to work on other musicals such as *Brigadoon* and *Gentlemen Prefer Blondes*.

Ninette de Valois had the vision and determination to see that a great national company could be developed in Britain. Born in Ireland in 1898 she performed in pantomime and various small companies before joining Diaghilev for two seasons. On her return to England she formed a school which gave rise to the Vic-Wells Ballet in 1931. In the following years the company grew until it received its Royal Charter in 1956 and became the Royal Ballet. She has also been influential in the formation of the national companies in Australia and Canada.

Serge Diaghilev is probably the most important figure in ballet this century. Born in Perm, Russia in 1872 his original passion was music, but through his contact with a group of artist friends, including the designer Benois, he was drawn to ballet. Tired of the restrictions of the Imperial Ballet, he organized a group to dance in Paris in 1909, including the dancers Pavlova, Nijinsky, Karsavina and the choreographer Mikhail Fokine. Diaghilev's greatest talent was to bring together dancers, artists, choreographers and musicians to create great works such as *The Firebird, Petrouchka* and *The Rite of Spring*. During the later years of his company he tried to please a fashionable audience which wanted new and outrageous ballets each season. Even he could not provide this. He died in Venice in 1929.

Isadora Duncan was pioneer of modern dance whose life was perhaps more extraordinary than her work. Born in America in 1877, she died in Nice in 1927 in a tragic accident when her scarf caught in the wheel of her car. Her main influence was to free dance of many restrictions of dress, style and expression. She wore flowing draperies, often very revealing, and danced dramatic solos. She performed in Russia in the first years of this century and was seen by both Fokine and Karsavina. Years later, after the Revolution, she accepted an invitation to found a school in Moscow. Her dances are almost forgotten, but her influence remains.

Margot Fonteyn is perhaps, after Pavlova, the greatest ballerina to bring ballet to a wide audience. She is not the typical, rather cold, ballerina, but has an appealing charm never shown better than in *The Sleeping Beauty*. Her life story has been told many times, never more simply than in her autobiography. At sixty-one she still makes occasional appearances though not in the great roles of the classics or those made for her by Frederick Ashton.

Martha Graham founded the most widely used style of modern dance which is now taught in many schools and is the basis of many companies. She formed her first groups to dance works in her newly created style as early as 1926, though what was then controversial is now accepted by a wide audience. Her company still perform her works and it was only in her seventies that she stopped appearing in them. At eight-six she still guides the fortunes of both her company and school.

Sir Robert Helpmann in the role of Doctor Coppelius. He excels in such character roles, but in the early years of British ballet he was expected to do almost everything moving from classical Prince to dramatic actor to comic character with remarkable versatility

Robert Helpmann was born in Australia in 1909, but made his name with the Vic-Wells Ballet in the 1930s. He created many great roles in the early years of the company as well as partnering both Alicia Markova and the young Margot Fonteyn. His range was great and he was an important figure in establishing male dancing in Britain. He appeared in films such as *The Red Shoes* and *Tales of Hoffmann.* He returned to Australia in the 1960s to create ballets for the young Australian Ballet there and directed it for a time. He still makes occasional appearances as one of the two Ugly Sisters, the bossy one, in Ashton's *Cinderella.*

Zizi Jeanmaire is one of the ballerinas who have helped bring ballet to a cinema audience, as well as dancing in stage shows and cabaret. Her first great role was in Roland Petit's *Carmen*, which she has recently filmed again, this time with Mikhail Baryshnikov. She still appears on stage at the age of 56, mostly in works like *The Bat* by Petit whom she married in 1954. He, too, made choreography for several films including *Hans Christian Anderson.*

Tamara Karsavina tells her own story in the charming book *Theatre Street.* Born in 1885 she graduated, partnered by Fokine, in 1902. By 1909 she had started her famous partnership with Nijinsky and she created such great roles as the Firebird in the ballet of the same name and the Doll in *Petroushka*. In later years she made an important contribution to British ballet by her dancing, in the 1930s, and after that by coaching other dancers such as Margot Fonteyn. She died in 1978.

Gene Kelly was born in 1912 and made his name on Broadway before going to Hollywood in the early 1940s. He introduced into dance an everyday casualness which was almost the opposite of Astaire's formal elegance. His most important early film was *On the Town*, the story of three sailors on leave in New York, which was inspired by Jerome Robbins's ballet *Fancy Free*. Later films included the brilliant *Singin' in the Rain* which also contains some excellent comic dancing by Donald O'Connor. In his style Kelly was unique, but his later attempts to become more balletic were not so successful.

Lincoln Kirstein was the founder of New York City Ballet with George Balanchine. Balanchine came to America in 1933 at his invitation and together they founded a school and then a company which eventually became N.Y.C.B. He is still co-director of the company and an important writer on dance.

Leonid Lavrovsky is perhaps most famous for his great ballet *Romeo and Juliet*, which he created at the Kirov Theatre in Leningrad in 1940 for Galina Ulanova. It became the prototype of the big heroic ballets we now think of as typical of the Bolshoi, such as *Spartacus* and *Ivan the Terrible*. He was also the father of the great dancer Mikhail Lavrovsky.

Serge Lifar was the last of the great dancers discovered by Diaghilev. He created the leading roles in both the great Balanchine ballets *The Prodigal Son* and *Apollo*. He was very important in restoring the ballet at the Paris Opera in the 1930s, in particular making the school important again. Born in 1905 he was always handsome and attractive on stage and made many ballets to show off his looks as well as his dancing. He is still a colourful personality on the dance scene.

Alicia Markova danced with the Diaghilev's

Ballets Russes at the age of fourteen in 1924 after studying with the great teacher Astafyeva. She created the role of the Nightingale in Balanchine's ballet of that name two years later. After Diaghilev's death she returned to England and danced with the young Ballet Rambert and created roles in the earliest Ashton ballets. She was the first true British prima ballerina and also the first to dance *Giselle* and Odette/Odile in *Swan Lake*. Her famous partnership with Anton Dolin eventually led to the creation of the London Festival Ballet. She now teaches and coaches extensively in Britain and America passing on her superb Romantic style.

Vaslav Nijinsky was perhaps the most famous dancer of all time. His life story has featured in books, films, theatre and ballets. He revolutionised male dancing, with his spectacular technique and oriental features, giving it an importance it had not had for over a hundred years. He also made a great impact with his ballets, *Afternoon of a Faun* and *The Rite of Spring* in which both his choreography and Stravinsky's music caused a riot at the first performances. He was born in Kiev in 1888 and died, after over thirty years of mental illness, in London in 1950.

Rudolf Nureyev made his great leap to freedom when he asked for asylum in the West in Paris in 1961. He made a terrific impact on audiences and on male dancing, during the 1960s. Given his example dancers of the Royal Ballet in particular took up the challenge with noticeable improvement. He was then 23 and already had made a great impact at the Kirov Theatre in Leningrad where he had received his training. His spectacular technique and Tartar looks cannot avoid a comparison with Nijinsky, nor can his impact on the public.

Anna Pavlova brought ballet to vast audiences all round the world. No place was too small or too far for her to take her gallant troupe of dancers. Born in St Petersburg in 1881, she died in The Hague in 1931. She wanted to become a dancer after seeing a performance of *The Sleeping Beauty* in 1890, found a place at the Imperial School in 1891 and had already appeared on the stage of the great Maryinsky Theatre (now the Kirov) before she graduated in 1899. She danced in the first Diaghilev season in

Ballet star Rudolf
Nureyev appeared on
The Muppet Show,
dancing *Swine Lake*
with Miss Piggy

Paris, but preferred to go her own way, forming her
own company. She eventually settled in London in
her beloved Ivy House, which now houses a museum
in her memory.

Marius Petipa dominated ballet in Russia for
over forty years. He was responsible for the creation
of the classical ballerina, made to shine at the centre
of his classic ballets. He was born in France in 1818
and died in Russia in 1910. He danced in his father's
company when young though he was overshadowed
by his brother Lucien. He found his real talent soon
after his appointment as Principal Dancer at the
Imperial Theatre in St Petersburg. He soon began to
choreograph and after the success of *The Daughter of
the Pharaoh* he was appointed ballet master, a post he

held until 1903. During this time he created the formula of the classical ballet seen at its greatest in *Swan Lake*, *The Sleeping Beauty* and *The Nutcracker*.

Roland Petit is particularly important for the revival of French ballet in the 1940s. He introduced important painters and designers into the theatre alongside his own highly theatrical choreography. His most famous ballets include *Carmen* and, more recently, *The Bat* and his own version of *Coppélia* for his company in Marseilles.

Marie Rambert was the great talent spotter in the early days of British ballet. She was born in Poland in 1888 and trained in early modern dance. Through this connection she was employed to help Nijinsky with his choreography for *The Rite of Spring*. She become interested in classical ballet and when she came to London she opened a studio which would eventually produce choreographers such as Frederick Ashton and Antony Tudor. The talent she discovered often went elsewhere, but she continued to find dancers and choreographers. Even when her small company became a modern dance company she encouraged young choreographers. One of her discoveries, Norman Morrice, is now Director of the Royal Ballet, others are creating ballets all around the world.

Jerome Robbins is perhaps the greatest American-born choreographer, working with both the great American companies and more than anyone else he has succeeded in blending ballet with Broadway. His own first ballet was *Fancy Free* which became the film, *On the Town*, and since then he has alternated between both worlds. On the ballet stage he has created ballets ranging from the funniest comic ballet ever, *The Concert*, to the wonderful dance work *Dances at a Gathering*. On the stage he produced one of the most important musicals of recent times, *West Side Story*.

Moira Shearer was born in Scotland in 1926 and had a brilliant career in the Sadler's Wells Ballet, being Margot Fonteyn's only real rival. She popularised ballet through her role in the greatest ballet film ever made, *The Red Shoes*, and with her striking red hair and beautiful looks was a ballerina, like Fonteyn, a modern audience could identify with.

Moira Shearer in the Ballroom scene from the film *The Red Shoes*. A beautiful dancer who enjoyed great fame on stage and film she married and gave up her career at the height of her powers

Igor Stravinsky was the most influential composer for ballet this century. He was born in Russia in 1882 and was brought into ballet by Diaghilev who heard some of his early pieces. Diaghilev eventually commissioned *The Firebird* from him, the first of a long line of exciting ballet scores which included, *Petrouchka*, *The Rite of Spring* and *Les Noces*. His collaboration with George Balanchine started with *Apollo* in 1929 and continued through ballets such as *Orpheus* and *Agon* up to his death in 1971.

Antony Tudor was born in London in 1909, the year that Diaghilev brought his company to Paris. Encouraged by Marie Rambert, he began making ballets for her company and created deep psychological characters which were a new challenge for dancers. In recent years he has created few works, but his ballets such as *Pillar of Fire, Lilac Garden* and *Dark Elegies* are all very moving works and still widely performed.

Agrippina Vaganova who was born in 1879 was a ballerina with the Imperial Theatre. She became interested in teaching, first in private schools and then at the Leningrad Choreographic School. It was through her work and her influence that the line of classical ballet was not lost in the years after the Russian Revolution in 1917 when there was strong opposition to it because of its connections with the Tsar. Her teachings have been written down and form the basis of many other classes. She continued teaching to the end of her life and her last pupil, Kolpakova, is still the radiant ballerina of the Kirov company. The school in which she taught was named after her, just six years after her death in 1951.

Edward Villella is an American dancer who was born in 1936, and along with his fellow dancer Jacques d'Amboise, has helped make dancing an acceptable profession for boys in America. His very athletic style and open personality appeal to a wide audience. He had particular success in Balanchine's *Prodigal Son* and the 'Rubies' section of *Jewels*. He dances rarely now, but still makes television and personal appearances lecturing on and demonstrating ballet.

Vera Volkova was an influential teacher from the time she left Russia, via Shanghai, in the 1920s until her death in 1975. When she reached London in the Second World War she opened a studio and influenced many rising young dancers, particularly Margot Fonteyn. She then went on to the Royal Danish Ballet adding her great experience of Russian technique to the traditional Danish style. Many of the Danish dancers of today, such as Peter Martins and Peter Schaufuss, were taught and coached by her.

Edward Villella, the American dancer, in *Tchaikovsky pas de deux* by George Balanchine

Acknowledgments

The illustrations are reproduced by kind permission of the following:
Malcolm L. Keep 1; Jesse Davis (Mike Davis Studios Ltd) 3, 7, 16
(bottom), 50, 55, 65, 75, 113; Peter Newark's Historical Pictures 4;
Society for Cultural Relations with the USSR 5, 28 (right); Victoria
and Albert Museum, London 6; BBC Hulton Picture Library 11; The
Mansell Collection 13, 86 (right); The Raymond Mander and Joe
Mitchenson Theatre Collection 16 (top), 26, 29, 59, 63; International
Museum of Photography at George Eastman House (Photo: Disderi)
19; National Portrait Gallery, London 20; Sovfoto/Eastfoto 23, 25;
Mary Evans Picture Library 24; Observer/Transworld 28 (left); Nigel
Luckhurst 32, 35, 41; Syndication International 38; Camilla Jessel 45,
69, 84; Novosti Press Agency (A.P.N.) 46–7; Klas Rickman 48; Leslie E.
Spatt 51, 96; Steven Caras 53; Sandy Underwood, Cincinatti, Ohio 56;
Paul Roylance 66–7; Mike Ralph (AVA Department, West London
Institute) 68; Lois Greenfield, New York 71; Otto M. Berk, New York
78; Metro-Goldwyn-Mayer Inc. 80; BBC Copyright Photograph 82; The
Press Association 86 (left); Gert Jangblom 89; Victoria and Albert
Theatre Museum (Photo: Gordon Anthony) 101; Robert Harding
Associates 103 (top); Kobal Collection 103 (bottom); Australian News
and Information Bureau 107; Associated Newspapers 110.